Black Teenage
Mothers

Black Teenage Mothers

Pregnancy and Child Rearing from Their Perspective

Constance Willard Williams

Lexington Books

D.C. Heath and Company/Lexington, Massachusetts/Toronto

Library of Congress Cataloging-in-Publication Data

Williams, Constance Willard.
Black teenage mothers : pregnancy and child rearing from their
perspective / Constance Willard Williams.
p. cm.
Includes bibliographical references.
ISBN 0-669-24313-2
1. Afro-American teenage mothers—Attitudes. 2. Teenage
pregnancy—United States. I. Title.
HQ759.4.W55 1990
306.85'6—dc20   90-41347
CIP

Published simultaneously in Canada
Printed in the United States of America
International Standard Book Number: 0-669-24313-2
Library of Congress Catalog Card Number: 90-41347

The paper used in this publication meets
the minimum requirements of American National Standard
for Information Sciences—Permanence of Paper
for Printed Library Materials, ANSI Z39.48-1984.

(∞)™

Year and number of this printing:

91 92 93 94   8 7 6 5 4 3 2 1

Contents

Tables

Acknowledgments

T he completion of this book would not have been possible without the encouragement and assistance of many people. Dr.
Janet Z. Giele, director of the Family and Children's Policy Center
at the Florence Heller Graduate School for Advanced Studies in
Social Welfare, Brandeis University, and the members of my committee, Norman Kurtz, Peter Conrad, and Deborah Klein Walker,
encouraged me to write this book based on my dissertation research.
Anne Groves and Angela Nicoletti along with the social workers
from their respective departments at Brigham and Women's Hospital, as well as Fran Kellog-Trautman of St. Margaret's Hospital for
Women, provided me with access to the young mothers who participated in this study.

Annette Macaudda spent many hours transcribing interviews.
Jean Layzer, a senior analyst at ABT Associates, read the manuscript and made many helpful suggestions about content and style.
Julia Gittleman, who is director of educational programs for Crittenton Hastings House, also commented on parts of the manuscript.

I am indebted to Dr. C. M. Newberger of Children's Hospital
Medical Center in Boston for her work on levels of parental concep-
tion, and to the Child Welfare League of America in Washington,
D.C. for permission to use the interview schedules developed by
Shelby Miller when preparing my interview guide.

My former colleagues at Boston College Graduate School of
Social Work—Dean June Gary Hopps, Robert Taylor (now at the
University of Michigan), and Regina O'Grady LeShane—were sup-
portive of my work in numerous ways.

Judith Gorbach and Saul Franklin at the Massachusetts Department of Public Health provided aggregate data from the state's Adolescent Pregnancy and Parenting Study.

I want to thank my husband, Preston, for his consistent support from the beginning of the study through the completion of the manuscript.

Finally, I gratefully acknowledge the thirty young mothers who participated in this study for opening their lives to me, and for their insights into the meaning of teenage birth and motherhood. Without their cooperation this book could not have been written.

Introduction

The idea for this study and its design developed during the time (1983–87) that I worked as the chief policy analyst in Governor Dukakis's Office of Human Resources. While in that position, I served as chairperson of the Statewide Task Force on Pregnant and Parenting Youth in Massachusetts. The task force was organized by the Alliance for Young Families, a coalition of agencies concerned about policies and programs for pregnant and parenting teens. My work with the task force confirmed the need for a clearer understanding of the point of view of teen mothers if we are ever to design successful policies and programs to delay or prevent teenage childbearing.

The issue of what aspect of teen pregnancy and childbearing to study was influenced by my personal interest in black female adolescent development and the public concern over births to unmarried black teenagers. Over one-half of all black births are to unmarried women and nearly half of all poor children are black. Poor young women who begin childbearing before age twenty are at great risk for remaining poor and never marrying. To address the problem, conventional wisdom advocates comprehensive sex education, birth control, and access to abortion and adoption. In the past, among black and white young women, the most common solution to premarital pregnancy was marriage. If no marriage occurred, it was common for black mothers to remain in the community with family or kin who assisted them in the upbringing of their children. The options of reliable birth control, primarily the pill, and safe legal abortions were not available to prevent unwanted pregnancies and births until the sixties and seventies; however, it is *since* the availability of birth control and abortion that increasing numbers of unmarried women, especially black and white teens of low socioeconomic status, have chosen to have babies and keep them. This raises the question of whether childbearing is perceived by the unmarried teenage mother as a problem. It is therefore advisable to examine more closely the motivation of this group of teenagers and what having babies means to them.

During the time that I was designing this study, several research reports and media events underscored the importance of pursuing this line of inquiry. Two are outstanding. First, a report on the impact of Project Redirection, (Polit, Kahn, and Stevens, 1985) a comprehensive service program for low-income pregnant and parenting teens, showed a high rate of second pregnancies among participants within a two-year follow-up period. This finding overshadowed other outcomes, and the program was judged a failure. The second event was Bill Moyers's controversial documentary entitled "The Vanishing Family—Crisis in Black America,"[1] which focused on the structure of the black family and the link between out-of-wedlock teen births, poverty, long spells on welfare, and the perpetuation of female-headed households. This documentary and the outcomes of Project Redirection supported the need to study teenage pregnancy and better understand the teen mother's perspective on the complex motivations that lead to childbearing among unmarried teenagers.

I decided to study second births as well as first births to teens because there is a great deal of research on teenage mothers with one child and hardly any research on second births to teenage mothers. Teenagers who have second babies may be better able to reflect on the meaning of the experience since they already know some things about being a mother that first-time teen mothers have not experienced. Therefore, the meaning of birth and keeping and rearing children can be more effectively explored if one does not rely solely on the experiences of first-time teen mothers. One may also discover whether or not teen mothers regard a second birth as a negative outcome.

The goal of the study was to understand the meaning of births to teenage mothers by analyzing interviews with a group of mothers who had borne two children as teenagers and another group who had borne one child during the teen years. The focus is on the experiences of pregnancy and childbearing among black adolescent females and how they relate to their cultural and personal circumstances.

Rather than viewing teen births as a violation of norms, acting out behavior, or the result of unconscious wishes to be pregnant or punish parents, I take the view that given present-day black community and family patterns, taken together with economic circumstances, early out-of-wedlock births and the establishment of mother-centered families are not surprising outcomes. As Ladner (1972) suggests, early childbearing for teenagers in these circumstances is an adaptive or a reasonable response to their social and cultural reality.

To understand their views on teenage motherhood, I interviewed thirty young mothers who began childbearing when they were sixteen years of age or younger. I present the findings in the voices of the teen mothers whenever possible. The chapter that follows links the concern about black teenage fertility to the larger controversy about black family structure. The second chapter discusses factors that contribute to the incidence of teenage pregnancy, and research and attitudes toward teenage pregnancy. Chapter 3 presents the current conventional wisdom and some alternative hypotheses about teenage childbearing. Chapter 4 describes the method and the sample. The next three chapters, 5, 6, and 7, focus on the teen mothers and constitute the heart of the book. The final chapter suggests research and policy implications.

Black Teenage
Mothers

1
Moynihan and Beyond

This chapter gives the history and background of a problem that has become of great concern in public policy—the high rate of childbearing among unmarried black teenagers. The intellectual history of this problem begins not with teenage pregnancy, which only became a public concern around 1970, but with worries about black family structure that began in the 1960s with the Moynihan Report (1965). Much of the subsequent research and public policy on black teenage pregnancy has been sidetracked by an emphasis on the public costs and personal tragedy of teen childbearing. The extent to which cultural influences, poverty, and racism shape the sexual and reproductive behavior of black adolescents have not been adequately discussed. What is now needed is a close examination of the actual lives of these young women—what blocks them and what motivates them—in order to make any real progress with the serious issues of poverty and welfare that surround the lives of many black teenage girls.

In 1965, Daniel Patrick Moynihan, assistant secretary of labor to President Johnson, wrote a report, "The Negro Family: The Case for National Action," popularly known as the Moynihan Report (Rainwater and Yancey, 1967). The report suggested that black families, operated on a principle contrary to the norm then held that the father was the head of the family: the black family was matriarchal. The black family was linked to and often determined by joblessness, illegitimacy, poverty, and a host of other issues confronting urban blacks. Moynihan's thesis that black youth were caught in "a tangle of pathology" that repeated itself generation after generation and perpetuated a woman-centered family structure was supported by census and labor market data. Numerous comparisons were made between white and black youth to show the differences between families with one parent present and families with both parents present. Low educational attainment, high crime rates, and unemployment among black males were shown to be associated with absent fathers. Moynihan drew attention to the unfavorable economic position of female-headed families, an association that would become commonplace during the seventies when family breakup was increasing and greater numbers of women were entering the work force.

There were strong negative reactions to the Moynihan Report. Because he spoke not only as a social scientist but as an adviser to the president, Moynihan's thesis was attacked as politically motivated rather than scientifically derived. The significance of the link between female-headed households and poverty was overshadowed by the political contest between blacks and President Johnson in the fight to eliminate racism. The larger contest obscured the fact that, for example, in Moynihan's analysis, black males were compared with black females, and black females were found to be better off in educational attainment and employment. This disparity between black males and females, according to Moynihan, was at the heart of the pathology facing the black family. Moynihan recognized discrimination as a factor in the educational and employment prospects of blacks, yet failed to spell out its implications. The failure to propose firmly educational and employment policies to correct conditions for blacks led to an emphasis on the black family as the problem. A comparison between the educational and job opportunities available to black males and those available to white males of comparable status might have focused attention on the restricted options and opportunities available to black males rather than on black family structure. Perhaps then the Moynihan Report might not have been perceived as blaming the black family for conditions that originated in the social structure.

While Moynihan drew on the works of E. Franklin Frazier, Kenneth Clark, Thomas Pettigrew, Robert Blood, and other well-known social scientists who had made similar observations about conditions facing blacks, none of these stirred controversy equal to that surrounding the Moynihan Report. None of these scholars carried out their studies while serving in political office, nor were any of them known to be politically ambitious. Though Moynihan was careful to point out that in spite of enormous odds, some black families became stable units, that the disparity between black and white intelligence scores and achievement was not due to genetic differences, and that discrimination was a factor in the employment opportunities of black males, the report was considered an insensitive and racist political document. Wilson (1987) argues that the "unflattering depiction of black family life" caused the report to be labelled racist and deflected the attention of social scientists away from the study of urban social problems for the next two decades. Another factor may have been Moynihan's political position and ambition, which were at odds with a totally disinterested stance as a social scientist.

Regardless of the political dimension of the Moynihan Report, it has become a landmark academic study and has been both praised and condemned by many scholars. William Ryan attributed methodological weaknesses and sweeping conclusions based on insufficient data to the Moynihan Report and characterized it as "a highly sophomoric treatment of illegitimacy" that neither addressed the differential reporting of illegitimate births among blacks and whites, nor paid adequate attention to the illegitimate conception rates among whites that were dealt with by shotgun marriages, abortion, and access to adoption and maternity homes (Rainwater and Yancey, 1967). Further, Ryan concluded that Moynihan attributed the conditions of black life to the "pathology" of the black family and the past history of enslavement rather than to present-day segregation and discrimination.

Laura Carper criticized the report for its failure to recognize that the matriarchal family form is more related to poverty than to race and is "a cultural formation common to many oppressed people throughout the history of western civilization" (Rainwater and Yancey, 1967: 471). According to Carper, one solution posed by Moynihan—that black males could find the education, discipline, and opportunity missing as a result of their family structure by entering the armed forces—bordered on the absurd and ignored the real solution—the acquiring of social and economic power. Among

several intellectuals who responded to the Moynihan Report, Gutman (1976) produced a monumental work that documented the
existence of intact black families during and following slavery, and
Stack (1974) lived among poor blacks in public housing and reported
strong networks of exchange and cooperation.

The controversy that followed the Moynihan Report, in addition to inspiring commentary and research such as that mentioned
above, brought into being an oppositional literature by blacks that
emphasized the strengths of black families. This literature was also
academic and policy oriented. Billingsley (1968), Hill (1972),
Ladner (1972), and Willie (1976) described the black family as re-
silient, egalitarian, strong, and nurtured by an extended kinship
network and religious values. Robert Hill described the system of
informal adoption of out-of-wedlock children as evidence of the
high value black families assign to children. These writings illumi-
nated aspects of black family life heretofore slighted in the literature
but did not change the reality of out-of-wedlock births. This body of
literature also played a crucial role in the focus of research on the
black family in years to come. It was not popular to analyze the
negative problems facing some black families for fear of falling into
the trap of racism or undercutting efforts to secure government aid
to eliminate racism; thus these authors emphasized the strengths of
black families.

Billingsley, Hill, Ladner, and Willie made important contributions to the understanding of the adaptive capacities of black families, the role of the extended family, and the role of the church as
mediator between a hostile society and the black family. Yet just
as Moynihan's analysis was interpreted as seeing all black families
as weak, oppositional scholars gave the impression that all black
families were strong religious units with supportive kin and friendship networks. Neither approach to black family life, although
adopted by persons desirous of being helpful to blacks, was not
particularly conducive to critical analysis of the problem of illegitimacy or teen pregnancy and parenting. Policy objectives and concerns for preserving certain images of the victim obscured the real
issues.

In commenting on this either/or approach, Elmer and Joanne
Martin, in their work on the black extended family, observe:

Black people, at least the ones we know, have always known, even if social scientists have not, that there were strong black families and terribly disorganized ones too, but never a consistent pattern of either-or. The black people we have talked to are also aware that, though many blacks developed a stable family life in slavery, slavery and poverty have put black families generally at a great disadvantage in becoming economically stable units in the American society. (Martin and Martin, 1978: 113)

The views espoused by Moynihan and the oppositional literature are themselves the products of policy advocacy, racism, and structural inequality. The interpretation of the history of blacks in America is fraught with racism and individualism. The myth that with hard work and industry blacks, like immigrant groups, could make it is a part of our history and perhaps lead Moynihan to suggest that the black problem was one of pathology. So strong was the desire to refute a long tradition of faulty analysis and proposals inadequate to address years of unequal access to opportunity that the picture of a strong extended family with religion as its core value and poor inner-city families who established intricate systems of bargaining and exchange was a welcome alternative to the bleak, pathological story told by the Moynihan Report.

Blacks at that time were engaged in a civil rights struggle that sought to overturn and point to societal causes of oppression. American citizens had just witnessed the civil rights movement, and there were visible signs of progress in the removal of discriminatory barriers. It was not readily apparent that these changes left a large segment of black Americans untouched. This belief that all blacks were beneficiaries of civil rights gains, together with the human tendency to believe good news and deny bad news and the reluctance of whites to risk being labeled racist "experts" who "study" blacks, resulted in the absence of critical research on the urban black family. Until the recent work of Wilson (1987), Moynihan's emphasis on the relationship of family structure to poverty and joblessness received little attention in the literature or in social policy proposals.

The Moynihan Report was a political as well as a social scientific study. It was initiated at a time of great tension between a positive, aggressive civil rights administration and a positive, aggressive civil rights movement. Despite the good intentions of both parties, controversy over political matters lead to a distortion of two important issues: the history of black family structure and black teenage pregnancy.

2

Facts about Teenage Pregnancy

S ince the early seventies, a good deal of attention has been focused on pregnancy and childbearing among teenagers. Ironically, the attention to the problem of teen births came after, not during, the period of the greatest increase in teen fertility. Between 1970 and 1983, the birthrate (number of births per thousands) for females between fifteen and nineteen years of age declined from 68.3 to 51.7 and for girls between ten and fourteen years of age, from 1.2 to 1.1.[2] This decline in births occurred while the number of sexually active teens increased. How, then, does one explain the growing importance of this issue in both political and academic arenas when one trend indicates that the problem is declining rather than increasing? The reasons for increased attention to teen fertility can be found in demographic, cultural, and economic factors associated with pregnancy and childbirth.

The post–World War II baby boom caused a rise in the birthrate that continued into the early sixties. The aging of baby boom babies during the seventies meant that the number of teenagers in the population was 43 percent higher than in the previous decade (Baldwin, 1985). Birthrates for most teens declined during the seventies, while both birthrates and numbers of births fell faster for older women, leading to a rise in the proportion of births to teens. Although the overall rate of childbearing among teens and in older women decreased, the rise in the proportion of births to teens brought attention to the issue of teen fertility, which generally falls outside the scope of models that explain fertility rates among married women (Zelnik, Kanter, Ford, 1981). Moreover, it was assumed that an increase in the number of unmarried couples living together would increase illegitimacy, but not unplanned births (Zelnik, Kanter, Ford, 1981).

Unplanned births among young unmarried women in the United States have reached proportions unknown in other industrialized countries. The problem is more serious for young teens than for older teens, and more serious for blacks than for whites. An examination of how teenage pregnancy and birthrates vary by age, race, and national boundaries is necessary for a fuller understanding of teenage childbearing as an American social problem.

Determining Factors

Age

Between 1970 and 1983 the birthrate increased for white girls between ten and fourteen years of age from .5 per thousand to .6 per thousand.[3] This is the only group of teens for whom there was an increase in the birthrate during this period. But between 1960 and 1980, pregnancy, abortion, and births to young teens rose. In 1960 births to teens under fifteen years of age totalled fewer than 7,500 (Baldwin, 1985). In 1981, of the 537,000 births to teens, nearly 10,000 were to girls under fifteen years of age (Foster, 1986). By 1985 the total number of teen births had dropped to 477,705 but the number of births to girls younger than fifteen had risen to 10,220 (Pittman and Adams, 1988). For every birth to a girl under fifteen in 1983 there were three pregnancies of which an estimated 54.2 percent ended in abortion (Pittman and Adams, 1988). The increased pregnancy rate among young teens is attributable to black teens beginning sexual activity earlier than other teens—nearly all births to those under fifteen are to black adolescents. Young teens are not as likely to use birth control as are older teens; moreover, black teens are not as likely to get abortions as are white teens.

Race

Since 1970, not only has the birthrate risen for white girls age ten to fourteen, but this pattern can also be observed among older white teens as well. In 1970, the birthrate for white teens between fifteen and nineteen years old was 57 per thousand compared to 148 for blacks.[4] In 1983, the birthrate for all U.S. women fifteen to nineteen years old was 52 per thousand. For white women between fifteen and nineteen, the rate was 44 per thousand, whereas black teens of the same age had a birth rate of 95 per thousand.[5] In spite of the comparatively higher rate of childbearing for black teens, it is important to note that since 1970 out-of-wedlock births have increased among black and white teens: the proportion of births to unmarried black teens to all births climbed from 63 percent in 1970 to 89 percent in 1983, while the proportion of all births to unmarried white teens increased from 17 percent in 1970 to 39 percent in 1983 (Wilson, 1987). Wilson calls these increases for both groups "staggering."

The increase for white teens represented a departure from previous patterns of fertility. It is this change for white teens that has caused teenage pregnancy to be viewed as something other than pathological or immoral behavior, which had been the dominant view as long as the climbing rates were associated primarily with black adolescents. This change in focus has not always served black teens well because of the tendency to de-emphasize aspects of the problem that are particular to racial isolation and poverty.

Nevertheless, a childbearing rate among black teens that is more than twice that of whites means that the problem of teenage pregnancy is seen as a black problem rather than a white problem. Black teens are only 14 percent of the teenage population, yet they account for 28 percent of all adolescent births and 47 percent of all births to unmarried teens (Children's Defense Fund, 1986).

Many persons in positions of leadership in the black community and some civil rights and black civic organizations have begun to address the issue of teenage pregnancy. Eleanor Holmes Norton, a professor of law at Georgetown University and former head of the Office of Equal Opportunity in the Carter administration, characterizes teenage pregnancy as the "most serious long-term crisis facing black America today"[6] (1986). In its 1984 annual report, the Urban League called the facts associated with early childbearing an "ominous trend." In the 1986 Urban League report, Joyce Ladner declares: "There is no other problem in the black community today that is more threatening to future generations of families than teen pregnancy, a problem of monumental proportions that is producing the woman child and man child on unprecedented levels. It is a problem that will affect three generations—the teen parents, their children, and the grandparents" (Ladner, 1986: 65).

As Ladner states, one cannot minimize the magnitude of the problem of teen childbearing and its long-term effects. And, as we have stated above, the problem is far greater for black teens than for white teens. Yet, when one looks at teens in other Western countries, as the Alan Guttmacher Institute has, one must consider cultural factors as part of the reason why teen pregnancy and parenting are serious social problems in the United States. The difference between birthrates among American white teens and their peers from other developed countries is similar to the difference between black and white teens in the United States. As a result, our attention is drawn to the need for a deeper understanding of the effects of class, culture, and economic circumstances on adolescent sexual and reproductive behavior.

Cultural Factors

Adolescent sexual and reproductive behavior are frequently discussed as if they were determined only by individual drives and peer influences. While both factors are important, perhaps even dominant, teenagers take their cues from a number of sources including adult behavior and the media. Thus a discussion of teenage pregnancy and parenting in the United States may benefit from a broader context. Comparisons between American teens and European teens and European women and American women provide this context.

Findings from a study of European and American women conducted by the Alan Guttmacher Institute (AGI) and summarized in the Spring 1988 issue of *Family Planning Perspectives* indicate that issues surrounding reproductive care and behavior in the United States are not confined to teenagers alone but are common to older women as well, especially those in their early twenties. This research is reported here to alert us to the possibility that problems associated with teen pregnancy and childbearing may be less related to age than to larger cultural factors such as attitudes toward sex, sex education, and the organization of our health care delivery system.

Teenage sexual behavior and reproductive patterns are seldom analyzed in the context of the sexual and reproductive behavior of women in other age groups. As a result, public debate centers on pregnant and parenting teens, as if they were a subgroup cut loose from the social and cultural contexts of the total society. Teenagers, while more heavily influenced by peers, are also influenced by the behavior of adults, particularly if that behavior appears to bring personal rewards that outweigh public sanctions.

Recent research by McLanahan and Bumpass (1988) proposes socialization and role model theories as the most plausible explanations for early childbearing. Based on the comparisons between American adults and European adults, and between American teens and European teens, the behavior of black and white teenagers may differ only in degree from the behavior of their adult role models.

According to comparisons between American teens of child-bearing age and teens from other industrialized countries, growing up in America, regardless of race, increases the chances of becoming pregnant before age twenty. In 1976, the Alan Guttmacher Institute (AGI) revealed that American teens had higher rates of adolescent childbearing than did their counterparts in Canada, Japan, and the USSR. A more extensive comparative study by AGI (Jones et al, 1985) of teenage pregnancy in thirty-seven developed countries indicates that teenage fertility and abortion rates are considerably higher in the United States than in any other developed nation.

The AGI study is helpful in pointing to the particularly American nature of the problem by comparing white American teens to white teens in other Western countries. American white teenagers have pregnancy, birth, and abortion rates higher than comparative rates for teens in any other Western nation. White American teens are twice as likely to become pregnant as Canadian or French teens, four times as likely as Swedish teens, and almost twice as likely as teens in England and Wales. The AGI survey has helped to focus discussion on the pervasiveness of adolescent pregnancy in the United States and has raised questions that challenge our approach to the problem.

The assumption that the availability of sex education and contraceptives may encourage rather than delay adolescent pregnancy is challenged by the European experience. The rejection of sex education in public schools and the recent controversy surrounding the availability of contraceptives in school-based clinics is partly related to this assumption. Compared to the United States, other countries are more open about sex, teach sex education in schools, and provide access to free or low-cost birth control (Jones et al., 1985).

This comparison between white American teens and white teens from countries influenced by Western culture raises the possibility that peculiar American attitudes about sex and the organization of health care in the United States influence teenage fertility. Therefore, when studying a subgroup of the population, whether it be all women under twenty or black teenage mothers, it is helpful to view that subgroup in its larger social context, and the AGI study comparing European and American women helps to place teenage reproductive behavior in this larger context. The study shows that there are major differences in contraceptive use, pregnancy, abortion, and child-bearing rates between American adults and adults in other countries just as there are among teens. American women, "especially those in their 20s," have lower rates of contraceptive use, fewer and less easily available contraceptive methods, and greater nonuse of birth control. Other countries, unlike the United States, integrate contraceptive care into the primary health care system and make services available at little or no cost to the consumer (Rosoff, 1988: 52).

Economic Factors

One factor associated with teen childbearing in the United States that was found to be absent in teenage mothers in European countries is severe poverty (Jones et al., 1985). Poverty among teen child-bearers is one reason, perhaps the major reason, for the growing concern about births to unmarried teenagers. The link between giving birth as a teen and the formation of a female-headed family dependent on welfare is most troublesome to policymakers. The economic disadvantage that results from early unintended child-bearing is compounded by continued unmarried status, subsequent births, and failure to enter the labor force. Although a causal link between teen childbearing and receiving welfare has not been documented, a large number of teen childbearers do eventually establish independent households and depend on welfare as a major source of income (Cutright, 1973; Bane, 1986b; and Wilson, 1987).

The primary source of income for poor female-headed households is Aid to Families with Dependent Children (AFDC). In 1982, Moore and Burt stated that over 50 percent of the AFDC and food stamp budgets are expended on households in which the mother was a teenager at the time of her first birth. Another estimate suggested that all U.S. families started by teenagers cost taxpayers $16.65 billion in AFDC, food stamps, and Medicaid in 1985 alone (Hayes, 1987: 206). Reliance on public assistance by single women and their children caused politicians, policymakers, scholars, and service providers to focus attention on the group believed most likely to become long-term recipients—teen mothers.

In summary, although the overall rate of increase in teen fertility had declined by 1970, cultural, demographic, and economic factors associated with teen childbearing came to the attention of policymakers and scholars. It came to light that the only group for whom the rate increased were white teens; that black teens, even with declining rates, had close to 30 percent of all babies born to adolescents and almost half of all babies born to unmarried teens; that fewer of these teens were getting married and more of them were keeping their babies, which was consistent with the previous behavior of blacks but represented a new pattern of behavior for whites; and that the economic consequences for mothers, children, and the welfare budget were serious.

Discovery of the economic disadvantages incurred by early childbearing fit comfortably with the growing research emphasis on economic consequences of changing family patterns, which was a frequent topic in the literature of the seventies and eighties (Cutright, 1973; Ross and Sawhill, 1975; Pearce, 1978; Cherlin, 1981; and Garfinkel and McLanahan, 1986). This literature on the economic status of female-headed households analyzed the effects of family breakup on the economic well-being of women and children. The focus was not on black female-headed households, whose formation was less a result of family breakup and more a result of the number of black women and teen mothers who would never marry. While economic consequences were more dire for black women (Wilson, 1987) and particularly black teen parents, researchers' emphasis on female-headed households protected them from a fate similar to Moynihan's, namely, the charge of racism.

Consequences for Research and Policy

In the meantime, since the Moynihan Report, conditions in the ghetto have worsened. Between 1965 and 1980, births to unmarried black mothers increased from 25 percent to 57 percent, and female-headed households climbed from 25 to 43 percent (Wilson, 1987). Unlike the sixties, conditions of black urban life in the seventies and eighties did not influence the research agenda of social scientists with a liberal approach to problems of the urban, black underclass. Consequently, the liberal emphasis on the plight of minority groups in the context of the larger society and advocacy for open opportunity structures, especially through governmental action was missing from the literature (Wilson, 1987).

These conditions did, however, attract conservatives such as Gilder (1982), Murray (1984), Mead (1986), and Novak (1987), who approach the issues identified with the black urban underclass, namely, violent crime, joblessness, teen pregnancy, and illegitimacy, from the classical conservative perspective that tends to hold individual values and habits responsible for these problems and excludes the larger society from analysis except to deplore the effects of governmental intervention (Wilson, 1987: 5).

This conservative ideology influenced the approach to teen pregnancy. The Reagan administration proposed chastity clinics and saying no, opposed abortion, and cut funds for family planning clinics. This approach to teen pregnancy occurred while a so-called "new consensus" on welfare emerged. Both liberals and conservatives joined together in supporting work for welfare mothers and the rigorous pursuit of absent fathers through federally required, improved state child support enforcement programs.

The leader for welfare reform in the U.S. Senate was Daniel P. Moynihan, senator from New York. Moynihan's public policy statements in the eighties called attention to family structure but from a perspective different from that of the Moynihan Report. His new emphasis was on children in poverty. In a set of lectures (Moynihan, 1986) at Harvard University, his emphasis was not on family structure directly but on the economic consequences of growing up in a poor family. Since the largest number of poor children reside in black female-headed households, Moynihan returned to the original subject of the Moynihan Report by addressing the growing poverty of children without explicitly discussing black family structure.

Twenty years later, with a conservative administration in power, the conditions depicted in the Moynihan Report have worsened. The political response in the eighties to the growth in female-headed households and dependence on AFDC was employment and training for single mothers and financial responsibility for absent fathers. Unlike previous attempts to reform welfare, this response represented "a new consensus" between liberals and conservatives on single mothers, work, and welfare. Liberals and conservatives alike, however, are genuinely puzzled about the prevention of teen pregnancy.

It is known that the majority of women are sexually active by the age of nineteen (Hayes, 1987), but older teens (eighteen to nineteen) do not generate the degree of concern that younger teens do. There is a vast difference in the emotional and physical maturity between fifteen- and eighteen-year-old women, therefore, a widely accepted goal of teenage programs is the delay of sexual activity. There is general agreement among professionals working to prevent teen pregnancy that teenagers with choices and future plans for education are more likely to delay sexual activity than teens who do not think that they have such options. The earlier the age at first intercourse, the longer the period of exposure to the risk of pregnancy. Since most young women do not use birth control at first intercourse, and wait up to eleven months after initiating sexual activity to seek birth control, postponing first intercourse could reduce the number of teen pregnancies (Hayes, 1987). Yet helping teens to delay intercourse may be a more unrealistic goal than teaching teenagers to use contraceptives before first intercourse.

The next logical strategy for teens who do become sexually active is to assure the availability of contraceptives. For some this strategy poses problems. For many who oppose premarital sex, providing contraceptives to teenagers is morally unacceptable. For others, providing contraceptives for teenagers is an intrusion on parental responsibility and involves professionals in decisions that belong to the family. Since the most effective contraceptives are medically prescribed, in the absence of universal health care, access and cost are issues. These issues are daunting enough, but even more fundamental is the question of why poor teenagers whose peers are having babies, who themselves were born to teen mothers, and who are not college bound or hopeful about job prospects should delay sexual activity or use birth control.

3
What We Think about Teenage Pregnancy

In considering teenage pregnancy, it is difficult to separate ante-cedents from consequences. Teenage mothers in later life tend to do less well economically than women who delay childbearing until their early twenties (Furstenberg, Brooks-Gunn and Morgan, 1987), yet the majority of teen childbearers are poor to begin with. Low educational attainment is associated with teen childbearing, yet many teen mothers repeated grades early in their school careers or dropped out before becoming pregnant. Many teen mothers depend on Aid to Families with Dependent Children (AFDC), yet many were members of AFDC families when they became pregnant. Inef-fective contraception is one of the few issues that is clearly an ante-cedent rather than a consequence of teen pregnancy.

Ineffective Contraception Is the Problem

Since a sizable proportion of women of childbearing age have at least one unintended pregnancy during their lifetime (Forrest, 1987), it is logical to conclude that women would welcome effective, safe, and convenient birth control methods. That such methods do exist and women still report unintended pregnancies suggests that the issue may be more complex than it appears to be on the surface. In spite of the complexity surrounding personal sexual behavior and the high rate of unintended pregnancies among nonteens, some propose contraception as the major solution to teen pregnancy. For example, a distinguished panel established by the Committee on Child Development Research and Public Policy of the National Research Council, proposes contraception as the major strategy for the reduction of unintended pregnancies:

> Because there is so little evidence of the effectiveness of the other strategies for prevention, the panel believes that the major strategy for reducing early unintended pregnancy must be the encouragement of diligent contraceptive use by all sexually active teenagers. Male contraception, as well as male support for female contraception, is essential. In light of the demonstrated effectiveness of contraceptive use, especially use of the contraceptive pill and condom, in achieving this goal—
>
> *The panel concludes that use of the contraceptive pill is the safest and most effective means of birth control for sexually active adolescents. Aggressive public education is needed to dispel myths about the health risks of pill use by girls in this age group, and contraceptive service programs should explore nonmedical models for distribution of the pill.* (Hayes, 1987: 7–8).

Effective contraception is one of three proposed strategies for achieving the panel's primary goal of pregnancy reduction and is suggested as the only strategy with a well-developed scientific base. Two other strategies, enhancing the life options of disadvantaged teens and delaying the initiation of sexual activity, are seen as desirable but less sure strategies for the prevention or reduction of pregnancies.

On close examination, however, one might conclude that while more is known about the effectiveness of contraception because it is measurable, it may be no more effective as a strategy than the other two for several reasons, some of which are implicit in the language of the recommendation.

A key proviso in the recommendation is the *diligent* use of contraceptives. Teenagers are known to be sporadic pill takers. Irregular use of the pill is related to the infrequent, irregular, and unpredictable nature of teenage sexual activity (Zelnik, Kanter, and Ford, 1981). Teenage women taking the pill often cease taking it if they lose a boyfriend and experience long intervals between intercourse. Taking a medication daily during periods of sexual inactivity seems wasteful to the young teenager whose cognitive development may not enable her to connect the possibility of becoming pregnant with infrequent intercourse.

The recommendation that male support for contraception be developed requires not only education of both males and females but also a significant change in gender relations as well. Further, male support for contraception assumes the presence of a level of communication, planning, and commitment between adolescent sexual partners that falls outside of current experience.

Some researchers (Zelnik, Kanter, and Ford) warn against putting high hopes on contraception as a solution to teenage pregnancy:

> It is as naïve as it is common to believe that the solution to the problem of teenage pregnancy is simply the availability of a new and better contraceptive, even one more suited to the particular needs of teenagers. If such a contraceptive were to appear, reasons for not using it would still exist. Davis (1972), in an insightful sociological analysis of premarital sex and pregnancy, relates changes in premarital sex and illegitimacy to changes in social control and social discipline. The development of new contraceptive techniques neither promotes nor prevents such behavior or the events that stem from it. (1981: 20)

Zelnik, Kanter, and Ford (1981) suggest that regular use of birth control by teenagers transcends personal habits such as diligence. Life-styles of teenagers and variations in how teens from different class backgrounds experience change in the larger social order are necessary contexts for understanding individual choices.

In a *New York Times* interview, Furstenberg, reflecting on the high rate of repeat pregnancy among participants in Project Redirection, commented that "the mere provision of family planning services and educational incentives for a short period of time will not reverse the life situation of the teenage mother"[7] Furstenberg's observation suggests that whatever the approach taken, assuring diligent birth control use is unlikely when services are offered late and for short periods of time, as is usually the case with current programs for teens.

Contraceptive services are usually offered by programs under medical auspices. In 1981, 56 percent of agencies offering family planning services were health departments and 13 percent were hospitals (Hayes, 1987: 8). Thus the National Research Council Panel recommends the involvement of nonmedical programs for pill distribution. The most logical nonmedical personnel for this task are school personnel, yet even where there are school-based clinics, contraceptive distribution is done outside the school. Before increasing effective dissemination of the pill, the panel suggests that myths about the risks of the pill must be dispelled through education. There seems to be a gap between scientific knowledge about the safety of the pill and young women's experiences. Weight gain or nausea as a result of taking the pill may not be perceived as a "myth" by a teenager who is preoccupied with physical appearance and personal comfort. Before some teens can accept medical findings that the pill is safe, difficulties experienced by young women with the pill, though minor to medical personnel, must be taken seriously. Still, the pill is the method preferred by teens who do use contraception, and research indicates that few teens report a lack of familiarity with or knowledge about where to obtain birth control (Zelnik, Kanter, and Ford, 1981).

Finally, teen use of birth control must be seen in relation to the behavior of women over twenty. As reported in an earlier section of this chapter, adult women in the United States are reported to have lower rates of contraceptive use than their European counterparts, just as American teens were found to be less effective contraceptors than European teens. Perhaps the same cultural influences are at work in the behavior of American teens and adults. Therefore, it may be advisable to view American teen contraceptive behavior in relation to American women's behavior regarding birth control. After all, teens are influenced by the behavior of older sisters, their mothers, and other adults. Whatever influences contraceptive patterns among women in general may also influence the behavior of teenagers.

In summary, contraceptive use by teens is one of the obvious and more dependable strategies for the reduction of unintended pregnancies. Its success, however, depends on factors outside of the influence of medical personnel and others who may distribute the pill in the future. Among these influences are cultural values, personal motivation, habits, socialization in the family and among peers, and the irregular pattern of teenage sexual relationships.

Poverty Is the Central Problem

Although some see ineffective contraception as the problem, others emphasize the relationship between teen pregnancy and poverty. Since unmarried teen mothers, like female heads of household of all age groups, are at high risk for being poor, it is a common belief that teen births cause poverty. In the following discussion, we will examine poverty as an antecedent to teen pregnancy as well as the relationship between births to unmarried teens and continued poverty status.

Unmarried mothers and their children are more likely to live in poverty than any other segment of the population. In 1984, nearly half (47.8 percent) of the poor in America lived in female-headed families (Moynihan, 1986). Whereas divorce is responsible for a share of households headed by women, an increasing proportion of female-headed families are formed because of out-of-wedlock births. In 1982, 38 percent of all out-of-wedlock births were to teenage women, and 78 percent of all black out-of-wedlock births were to teen women (Wilson, 1987: 37). According to Lester Thurow, "Poverty is going to rise as long as the number of female-headed households rises, and they are rising very rapidly. In 1984 female-headed households grew twice as fast (2.6 percent) as the total number of households (1.3 percent)."[8]

Blacks are more likely than whites to live in a household headed by a female. In 1979, 35 percent of all blacks but 60 percent of the black poor lived in female-headed families, whereas 9 percent of all whites but 26 percent of the white poor lived in female-headed families (Bane, 1986a). Bane makes a distinction between the feminization of poverty in black and white families. Whites are subject to "event-caused" poverty caused by split-ups or the formation of a female-headed household, whereas blacks are subject to "reshuffled" poverty as a result of moving from a poor family of origin into another poor family constellation. For blacks being born into a poor family is a more prevalent cause of continuing poverty than having the family split up. For black poor teens who become parents and stay in their parents' household, becoming a teen mother does not cause poverty but may exacerbate an already economically strained situation. Bane reminds us "that only about a fifth of the poverty among black female-headed and single-person households appears to be driven by the events of household composition changes. Among blacks poor female-headed and single-person households are much more likely to be formed from households that were already poor" (Bane 1986a: 231).

The poverty of female-headed households formed by teen mothers, then, cannot be attributed solely to their unmarried status. It is linked to the fact that they come from poor households in the first place and their low educational attainment leads to lower earning power. Teen mothers who do work, work longer hours, have lower incomes and larger families than other young mothers (Moore and Burt, 1982). Thus, even with full-time work, it is difficult for teen parents to sustain a family. Jobs available to high school dropouts, and even high school graduates, rarely provide income above the poverty level. Further, such jobs do not provide health coverage, a benefit for which AFDC recipients are eligible.

Given the poor economic prospects of teen mothers, their dependence on AFDC following the birth of a baby, and the relative advantage of welfare over work at poverty wages, one might expect that women who bear children while in their teen years would remain on welfare. Findings from one longitudinal study indicate that the lasting effects of teen childbearing may be overstated.

> A substantial proportion of adolescent parents manage to recover from the handicaps imposed by early parenthood. Studies of teenage parents in later life show that many women have not followed the predictable course of lifelong disadvantage, even if they are not doing as well as their peers who postponed parenthood. Moreover, some portion of the adverse consequences presumed to be the result of early childbearing is, in fact, attributable to prior differences in the family backgrounds of early and later childbearers. When these differences are taken into account, the relative size of the disadvantage resulting from the timing of the first birth will diminish. The failure to take account of preexisting

differences may have led to an overestimation of the impact of premature parenthood on the life course of women. (Furstenberg, Brooks-Gunn, and Morgan, 1987: 9)

Most information about families formed by unmarried teens is based on research carried out soon after the birth of a first child. Programs for pregnant and parenting teens usually follow participants for two years after they give birth. As a result, little is known about the long-term effects of early childbearing. An exception is Furstenberg's longitudinal study of teen mothers in Baltimore. The study began in the mid-sixties with follow-up in 1972 and in 1984. Furstenberg found that pregnancy in early adolescence adversely affected the economic position of young mothers when compared with their classmates five years after the birth of a child, yet by the time of his second follow-up women had shown considerable "recovery" and "were living on incomes that provided at least a modest level of security" (Furstenberg, Brooks-Gunn, and Morgan, 1987).

Marriage and the number of children are the factors that seem to have had the greatest impact on economic status. Women who remained single parents had great difficulty carrying out the responsibilities of parenthood and employment. Remaining single and having two or more children was highly correlated with receiving welfare. Even though welfare is not necessarily permanent, Furstenberg found that about 70 percent of the women in his study used welfare for short periods and that chronic welfare dependency was the exception among the women. This finding is consistent with the work of Bane and Ellwood (1983), which documents that only a minority of the welfare population stays on welfare for long periods.

In addition to an interest in the effects of early childbearing on teen mothers, a growing body of research has developed regarding the well-being of children of teen parents. Hofferth and Hayes (1987) review this research and finds the following: health outcomes for infants of adolescent mothers are not related to the mother's age but to adequate prenatal and perinatal care; the mother's age seems to affect the child's intelligence and school performance, yet the direct effects are quite small and most of the difference is attributed to indirect effects such as family structure, maternal education, and family size; socioemotional and cognitive differences between children of adolescent mothers and those of older mothers were less related to age than family structure, and; no consistent relationship was found between the mother's age and child abuse and neglect.

Furstenberg, Brooks-Gunn, and Morgan (1987) also looked at the adolescent children who had been born to teen mothers in the Baltimore study. One very significant finding is the relation between school performance of the mothers and their children. School failure was identified as a risk factor in early childbearing. Teen mothers who were behind in school when they became pregnant had "dismal prospects for recovery" (Furstenberg, Brooks-Gunn, and Morgan, 1987: 151). Therefore, the discovery that half the children of the teen mothers in the study were behind in school is a troubling finding.

In summary, the future of adolescent mothers and the well-being of their children seem to depend less on the age of the mother at first birth than on other factors such as the teen mother's education, family structure, and family support. Mothers who begin childbearing as teens have poorer economic outcomes than older childbearers, and even though many "recover" in later life, the economic effects of early childbearing are not erased. As Furstenberg et al. (1987) suggest, the effects of early childbearing may be exaggerated, but early childbearing, especially together with disjointed family structure and poor educational attainment, can result in adverse effects on teen mothers and their children.

What, Then, Is the Problem?

Ineffective contraception, poverty, and the fact that many teen mothers improve their lives over time are important aspects of the teenage pregnancy and parenting issue. But all these factors tend to distract attention from identifying solutions for lowering pregnancy and birthrates among teenagers in the highest risk groups. The expectation that teenagers will become more diligent contraceptive users is more than we have come to expect from women over twenty. Married women with low socioeconomic status and young middle-class women with access to birth control are known to be poor contraceptors (Rainwater and Weinstein, 1974; Luker, 1975).

The working-class white women studied by Rainwater had a life-style and culture that placed a high value on children and considered having children the "natural" thing to do, even when additional children meant tightening economic circumstances. The young women studied by Luker weighed the costs and benefits of their behavior and were willing to risk pregnancy and obtain an abortion rather than diligently use contraceptives. Teen women, without the advantages of maturity, regularity, and privacy in their sexual lives, can hardly be expected to plan ahead and to behave in a rational manner when these traits are absent in many other groups of women.

While increasing access to contraceptives, particularly in non-medical settings, may have some impact on the teen pregnancy rate, it is unlikely that teens from communities where early sexual behavior is accepted in the peer group and the community (Hayes, 1987) will become more diligent users of contraceptives. There is little evidence that ignorance or lack of availability of birth control are reasons why teenagers do not use contraceptives, but there is ample evidence that social and cultural factors influence attitudes and behavior related to all aspects of reproductive behavior (Ladner, 1972; Rainwater and Weinstein, 1974; Stack, 1974; Gabriel and McAnarney, 1983; Hogan and Kitagawa, 1985).

Concentrating on the poverty of pregnant teens and their families tells us a great deal about the consequences of being poor and staying poor. Pregnancy does not cause teens to be poor. A more plausible explanation for rising poverty rates among female-headed households is the erosion of the worth of the welfare grant by inflation. AFDC, unlike retirement benefits, Supplemental Security Income, and widow's benefits, does not have built-in cost of living adjustments. Discussion regarding the economic status of unmarried teens focuses on welfare dependency and the fact that unmarried mothers and their children create a public burden. There is considerable public concern about welfare expenditures disproportionately allocated to long-term recipients who start having children while in their teens. According to Mary Jo Bane (1986b), data simply do not support the anecdotes that welfare is an incentive to start families. Three-fourths of teen mothers live with their own mothers and show little evidence of deciding to become mothers to establish their own households or of having made a financial calculation before having a child (Bane, 1986b). Perhaps one of the reasons the argument that poor women have babies to increase welfare payments stays alive is the lack of understanding of subcultures that place a high value on childbearing without requiring that it occur only after marriage or when one can "afford" to have children.

Adolescent members of these subcultures may not view with the same alarm as the dominant culture the birth of children during the teen years. It is well known that most teen mothers are daughters of teen mothers. Typically mothers do not want their daughters to make the same mistake they did, however, the daughter sees her mother long after she has "recovered" from the experience of early childbearing and the consequences may not seem so terrible. Mothers who were themselves teen mothers may find it especially difficult to counsel their daughters to resolve a pregnancy by aborting or giving up a child. After all, the mothers of the teens have coped, and as Furstenberg, Brooks-Gunn, and Morgan (1987) indicate, relatively well.

They cope, however, in a world in which it is difficult for parents to maintain control over children, in declining neighborhoods, and in a world of blocked opportunities. Under these circumstances there may be no compelling reasons to delay having a baby.

The Missing Text of Adolescent Pregnancy

Parental Control

The major tasks of adolescence are to avoid role diffusion and to establish personal identity (Erikson, 1968). The natural laboratory for accomplishing these tasks is within the peer group, which means that teens need to distance themselves from the family that prior to adolescence has been their primary reference group. Identification with the peer group, coupled with the process of becoming independent, signals a critical turning point for teenagers and their families. Parents lose the authoritative role they may have previously held, and parental control over the adolescents' ideas and physical movement decreases.

Normal tasks of adolescent development are not the only factors that lessen parental control. Goode (1982) identifies parents' loss of control over access to jobs or land as partly responsible for loss of control over decisions about the marriage and the timing and circumstances of childbearing of their own children. Lasch (1977) attributes a decline in parental authority to the permissiveness of the larger society and the decline of the father's role in the American family. All parents face these influences, but black inner-city parents face additional circumstances that undermine parental control.

Lasch's observation on the decline of the father's role in American families refers to two-parent families. For a majority of black children, there is no question of the declining role of fathers because their fathers are absent altogether. It is estimated that of all children born today, over half of them will spend some time in a female-headed household. This includes children whose parents marry, divorce, and remarry. For the majority of black children, perhaps all of their childhood, not just part, will be spent in a female-headed household. Blacks are more likely to remain single parents because of decreasing prospects for marriage (Wilson, 1987). Even if more black teen mothers married, the high rate of dissolution of teen marriages would still lead to the formation of female-headed households. What has changed for an increasing number of black women over the past two decades is that they may never marry (Furstenberg, Brooks-Gunn, and Morgan, 1987; Wilson, 1987).

A growing body of research shows that family upbringing is the most significant determinant of teenagers' attitudes and behavior in matters of sex, contraception, pregnancy, family formation, and family breakup (Zelnik, Kanter, and Ford, 1981; Hogan and Kitagawa, 1985; McLanahan and Bumpass, 1988). While family type does not determine the quality of family life in all cases, sociologically "ideal" families, according to Zelnik, Kanter, and Ford (1981), have a better chance of protecting and supervising teenagers. Black teens were found to be concentrated in the least ideal types of families, that is, single-parent, female-headed families and substitute families. In comparing family types of black and white children, Edelman (1987) found that black children were twice as likely as white children to live in institutions, three times as likely to live in female-headed households or be in foster care, four times as likely to live with neither parent and be supervised by a child welfare agency, and twelve times as likely as white children to live with a parent who has never married. When one parent is present or, as is the case in many of the living arrangements of black children, no parent is present, the socialization of the child suffers. McLanahan and Bumpass (1988) found that parental supervision and parental role models had a major influence on women who had grown up in one-parent families: these women were more likely to bear children early, have premarital births, and have their marriages breakup.

Families reflect what is going on in the larger society and particularly the immediate environment. Therefore it is necessary to examine the neighborhoods and social networks of black female-headed households and the teenagers who grow up in them.

Neighborhoods and Social Networks

A body of literature has developed that analyzes teenage pregnancy and other signs of social dislocation among poor blacks in terms of the decline in inner-city neighborhoods. The isolation of black city neighborhoods created by the departure of middle-class blacks and the decline in the basic institutions of family, church, and school, has left behind an underclass, a heterogeneous grouping of inner-city families and individuals whose behavior contrasts to that of mainstream society (Hogan and Kitagawa, 1985; Lemann, 1986; Wilson, 1987). Wilson is the major spokesman for this perspective. He has analyzed data from the Michigan Panel Study of Income Dynamics (PSID) to document changes that have occurred since 1970 in several central cities with significant black populations. Wilson has found a rise in welfare dependency, teenage pregnancy, out-of-wedlock births, female-headed households, and crime—indicators associated with the phenomenon of a rising underclass among blacks in five central cities: New York, Chicago, Los Angeles, Philadelphia, and Detroit.

The complexity of these problems does not lend itself to a single explanation but is the result of interrelated societal, demographic, and neighborhood variables (Wilson, 1987: 30). According to Moore, Simms, and Betsey, "the joint effect of living in a neighborhood with a high dropout rate and high unemployment and being a member in a low-income, single-parent household, may be considerably stronger than the effect of the three factors occurring separately" (1986: 139).

Racism, observes Wilson, is too facile an explanation. Ironically, the problems listed above increased the most significantly at a time when the country made its greatest strides against discrimination through affirmative action and other means. During the seventies, both black crime victims and perpetrators increased. The number of households headed by black women increased by 108 percent. In 1965, 24 percent of black births were out-of-wedlock; by 1982, 57 percent of all black births were out-of-wedlock. The above are a fraction of the changes cited by Wilson that indicate the magnitude of social dislocation in black inner-city neighborhoods.

Wilson proposes that historic discrimination, in combination with demographic and economic factors, offers a better explanation for the decline in the inner city than racism alone. Among the demographic factors, age is a key variable. Between 1960 and 1970, the population of central city blacks between the ages fourteen to twenty-four rose by 78 percent compared with an increase of 23 percent among whites of the same age (Wilson, 1987: 36). This concentration of black youth in central cities accounts partly for the high teen birthrate, high crime rate, and lower economic status of blacks. The age structure of the population is especially important in trying to explain the rise in female-headed households, because women under twenty-four years of age have higher sexual activity rates and higher birthrates.

Among the economic factors affecting social dislocation in central cities is the simultaneous increase in the minority population and decrease in the need for unskilled workers. Poor job prospects for blacks are due to what Wilson calls the "mismatch" between those needing jobs and the kinds of jobs being created. A black unskilled labor pool is jobless while jobs that require higher education and technical skills go unfilled.

Taken together, these demographic and economic factors partly explain the plight of the black underclass and cause "concentration effects" and social isolation: "the communities of the underclass are plagued by massive joblessness, flagrant and open lawlessness and low-achieving schools, and therefore tend to be avoided by outsiders.

Consequently, the residents of these areas, whether women and children of welfare families or aggressive street criminals, have become increasingly socially isolated from mainstream patterns of behavior" (Wilson, 1987: 58).

Wilson defines social isolation as "the lack of contact or of sustained interaction with individuals and institutions that represent mainstream society" (Wilson, 1987: 60).

The costs of isolation are high. One of its major effects is the removal of the jobless black male from a network of working people who know about employment opportunities and pass this knowledge on to others. In the absence of such networks, a reliance on welfare and the underground economy replaces jobs (Wilson, 1987: 57).

Blocked Opportunities

Demographic changes in the inner city and a decline in manufacturing jobs have led to fewer opportunities for black males and females to become economically self-sufficient. For black males this lack of opportunities has meant unemployment. Unemployed men are in no position to marry and support a family. Therefore, for black females with children, welfare is the primary source of income.

Black Male Unemployment. The "mismatch" in the available labor pool and the jobs that need filling requires a closer examination. Wilson compared the labor force participation between 1940 and 1983 of black males with that of white males and found that the labor force participation of white males remained stable or increased while it decreased for black males: "the proportion of black men who are employed has dropped from 80 percent in 1930 to 56 percent in 1983" (1987: 82). This means that employment opportunities for black men were greater during a time of high unemployment and greater segregation and racial discrimination. Since the thirties, the whole job structure in America has changed as a result of a decline in manufacturing and a decline in major industries such as steel and automobiles.

Those groups among black males most vulnerable to joblessness are black male teenagers and young black male dropouts. Wilson observes that in 1979, when the overall unemployment rate was 5.8, black male teens had an unemployment rate of 34.1 percent, but many teenage males could have still been in school. According to the Children's Defense Fund (CDF), black males between the ages of twenty and twenty-four "provide the clearest picture of how young men are faring in the labor market" (CDF, 1987). Young men in this age group who were high school dropouts suffered a 42 percent decline in annual earnings between 1973 and 1984, with the result that only one in nine black dropouts in this age group earned enough by 1984 to support a family. CDF reminds us that fathers of children born to teenagers are often in their early twenties, consequently, their educational level and employment prospects are related to the economic well-being and marriage prospects of teen mothers.

Wilson (1987) reviews a well-known body of literature that shows a relationship between employment and marital stability. Marital stability is adversely affected by unemployment, and a deterioration in marriage and family can be observed during times of high unemployment. He concludes from his review that joblessness in black men is the major factor in the rise of black female-headed households.

Using trends in male joblessness combined with male mortality and incarceration rates, Wilson constructs a "male marriageable pool index". "Clearly, what our 'male marriageable pool index' reveals is a long-term decline in the proportion of black men, and particularly young black men, who are in a position to support a family" (Wilson, 1987: 83).

Contrary to popular belief, Wilson concludes that welfare is not the major cause for the increase in black female-headed families, rather changes in the age structure have increased the fraction of births born to very young women. The proportion of births to unmarried women has in turn increased the number of female-headed households. Other contributing factors are black women's tendency to delay marriage and a lower rate of remarriage among black women.

Tom Joe (1987), has made a similar analysis: "It is reasonable to hypothesize that the erosion of the black family is not a mystical cultural trend but a palpable economic event. The boom in black

female-headed families is not simply the result of the "welfare
curse," of pervasive and invidious discrimination or of changing
sexual mores. Instead, the problem springs from an intricate economic and social dynamic. The anomie of black men is the product
of subtle social and economic cues that we have barely begun to
decipher" (Joe, 1987: 74–75).

With marriageable black men in short supply, it is not surprising
that black female teenagers neither marry, nor do they have high
expectations regarding marriage, nor do they believe that marriage
must precede pregnancy and birth. The economic circumstances of
black males provide the context for a fuller understanding of black
teenage childbearing.

Positive Reasons for Having a Baby. In the preceding section, we
have shown that the increase in female-headed households and
families headed by women who have never married is related to joblessness in black males. Researchers have disproved the notion that
welfare causes the formation of female-headed households or that
welfare is an incentive for teenagers to have babies. What, then, may
be the teenagers' reasons for having a baby?

The literature on teenage childbearing is filled with articles on
the consequences of teen childbearing. Titles and phrases such as
"children having children" and "risking the future" connote irre-
sponsibility and imply that postponing childbearing would enhance
future opportunities. One might ask, Does the teenager share this
view? The answer is, probably not. Black teenage parents usually
live with their mothers who themselves were teen parents. They
attend school and live in neighborhoods where their peers are teen
mothers. Given the time spent in school, at home, and in the neighborhood, a case can be made that this environment constitutes the
"world" of the black teen mother—the milieu in which her major
socialization occurs. In this world, the future is not filled with
opportunities.

Marini (1984) suggests that preferences about acceptable behavior are products of socialization based on the internalization of the
behavior pattern of significant others. Teenage pregnancy is often
discussed in relation to societal norms and from a life course perspective rather than in relation to influences of a subculture. Marini

proposes that teen pregnancy be evaluated in terms of a range of acceptable behavior rather than conformity to norms. The behavior of significant others, particularly mothers and peer group members, suggests to black teenage women that having a baby while young and unmarried is not only acceptable but expected. Expected behavior is based on customs—what one will do—rather than on norms, which involve a collective evaluation of what one ought to do (Marini, 1984). In the context of their families and peer groups, black teens are likely to see early childbearing as conforming to behavior that is customary and possibly expected rather than as deviating from an accepted norm or a proper sequencing of events.

As the preceding section indicates, males encountered by black teenage females are not likely to appear marriageable in the foreseeable future; therefore, in terms of economic security or marriage, having a baby jeopardizes neither. We have pointed out that teen mothers are not made poor as a result of childbearing, and instead usually come from poor households. Thus, it is unlikely that they see having a baby as leading to negative economic consequences.

Having children because children are intrinsically valuable or because women throughout history have had children as a natural part of life that satisfies biological and emotional needs is seldom mentioned as an explanation of teen childbearing. Yet in a culture where infertile women go to great expense to bear a child, the importance of having one's own child is dramatized by the use of surrogate mothers whose biological mates are not sociological fathers. The well-known Baby M case also illustrates that surrogate mothers may not find it easy to give up a biological child. Yet many people cannot understand why adoption is not popular among teen mothers. Teenagers, although primarily influenced by their immediate surroundings, are also influenced by what is happening in the larger society, which may lead them to conclude that having a child of one's own is as highly valued outside of their peer group and neighborhood as it is inside.

Finally, teenagers who have children are unlikely to have a variety of educational and employment options. Thus, a usual recommendation made by people who study teenage childbearing, is that the life options available to adolescents be increased. In the absence of an array of options regarding the future, having a baby could be the one thing that the teen mother hopes will give meaning and purpose to her life. Little research on teen mothers is done from this perspective, but there is a sparse but relevant body of literature from an insider's perspective.

Throughout this chapter, demographic, economic, and cultural aspects of the world of black teen mothers have been described. But the dominant view expressed is the perspective of the outsider looking in. Though not numerous, some studies have approached the topic of teenage pregnancy and births to young mothers from the teenager's point of view.

The World of the Black Teenage Mother

Ladner's (1972) ethnographic study of teenagers living in an urban housing project during the sixties sought to understand the meaning of becoming a woman from the perspective of black preteen and teenage girls. A part of their conception of being a woman was related to childbearing:

> The anticipation of womanhood is symbolized by certain types of acquired characteristics that are felt to render independence. One of these independent characteristics is the belief by some of these preadolescents that having a baby will achieve a certain kind of responsibility for the girl, and consequent womanhood, that she could not otherwise enjoy. The acceptance of having a baby as a symbol of womanhood was expressed by girls of all ages ... Twelve-year-old Terri told me that she wanted to give birth to a child when she reached sixteen or seventeen because she felt that it would give her some "responsibility." When I inquired as to what kind of "responsibility," and why was it felt necessary, the reply was that her older sister had had a child at sixteen, and she was now a "responsible" adult. (Ladner, 1972: 128)

Terri's notions about womanhood were clearly shaped by her immediate environment: her role model came from her family. Ideas about what she could be and what it was desirable to be were based on the behavior of significant others in her life. Whereas many of the teens Ladner interviewed thought that having a baby out-of-wedlock was a "mistake," no shame was associated with having a baby, and neither the teenagers' family nor the community attached a stigma to having a baby out-of-wedlock.

Ladner interpreted that the behavior of the teens represented a healthy adaptation to unhealthy environmental conditions (Ladner, 1972: 13). They were using coping and "survival" strategies in the face of poverty. Ladner called attention to high black male unemployment and the independent role of the female who was often left to support herself and her children. Later, in an article for the Urban League (1986), Ladner did not stress the adaptation made by black teens but called attention to the serious nature of teen pregnancy and viewed it as "threatening future generations" of black families rather than representing a survival strategy.

Ladner's early work succeeded in providing an insider's perspective on pregnancy, childbearing, and other aspects of life for poor black women. Her work fits into the tradition of the post-Moynihan literature that aimed to set the record straight about the forces of racism and discrimination that impinge upon black families.

Stack (1974), lived among black families in a large public housing project in St. Louis, which she named The Flats. Here she observed an easy and natural orientation to out-of-wedlock births and described a wide kin network that participated in parenting children of young mothers, which resulted in a child having several "parents." Like Ladner, Stack viewed the strategies employed in child rearing as adaptations for survival. Stack's work also fits the category of examining black family life to discover its strengths and resilience.

From my experience with social work clients in Boston Public Housing in the early seventies, extensive kinship and friend networks of exchange were not apparent, but an aloofness and suspicion was often present. This difference could be due to the fact that The Flats were located in the Midwest, not in the high-rise impersonal structures characteristic of Northern public housing. In the aftermath of the Moynihan Report, Stack may have made observations that were not generalizable to all sections of the country. The extended family network in evidence in Stack's study has diminished in the families of the underclass described by Wilson in the eighties.

Following the research tradition of Ladner and Stack, Schwab's participant-observer study (1983) of white, rural teens in New England sees them as attempting to cope with "poverty, lack of self-esteem, socialization for dependence on a male, socialization for motherhood as sole adult female identity, lack of independence, whether due to lack of mobility, money, or alternative roles and activities, and insufficient availability of training for gainful employment" (Schwab, 1983: 311). In light of these circumstances, Schwab, like Stack and Ladner, concludes that childbearing is adaptive behavior, a rational response to the teenager's cultural and socioeconomic reality. Although Schwab sees this behavior as adaptive for the teen, she concludes that it is not adaptive for the social environment and the children who are the "incidental effects" of the teenagers' adaptive behavior (1983: 231).

A recent study by Speraw (1987) explores adolescent perceptions of pregnancy among white, black, Hispanic, and Pacific-Asian teens enrolled in educational programs. In her literature review, Speraw notes the absence of cross-cultural studies from the adolescent's perspective (1987: 181). With the exception of a small sample of interviews carried out as a part of a larger program evaluation study of Project Redirection (see Levy and Grinker, 1983: 226), I found no other research based primarily on teenagers' perspectives.

Black teens in Speraw's study were pleased to be pregnant, found pregnancy not to be disruptive, expected motherhood to be a positive experience, were happy to have something of their own, did not feel guilty, and had strong support from their families. Speraw stated that her study confirmed findings in existing literature that a high value is placed on children in the black community. In comparison, white teenagers in Speraw's study gave more egocentric responses and reflected guilt feelings and perceived social isolation (1987: 193).

In summary, research on teen pregnancy and birth from the perspective of the teen mother is only a tiny part of the prolific literature on teen pregnancy and parenting. Early studies by Ladner and Stack emphasized the adaptive and survival aspects of early childbearing in the black community. They did not foresee the steady increase in out-of-wedlock births. Ladner discussed unmarried motherhood in the context of the black community and observed that there were no "illegitimate" children. Stack documented the existence of many sociological parents who participated in a wide kin and friend network to assist the young mother in parenting.

Stack somewhat romanticized ghetto life. Her experience in the Midwest was not common to that of large, impersonal, high-rise Northern public housing projects. Yet both Ladner's and Stack's portrayals of black inner-city families also bear some similarity to Wilson's description of joblessness, poverty, and female-headed households. The magnitude of these problems, however, was not as great in the seventies as it is today. In 1987 Wilson painted a much more serious picture of declining neighborhoods and joblessness, which have an enormous impact on the daily lives of individuals and families.

4
Method and Sample

This study is based on in-depth interviews with thirty young mothers who gave birth between the ages of fifteen and eighteen. The focus of the interviews is the exploration of the meaning of pregnancy, childbirth, and being a mother from the perspective of the teenager. Unlike most studies, this research includes mothers with two children as well as mothers with one child. The purpose of including mothers with two children is to focus on a population about whom researchers and policymakers express great concern but have little information. Second births have seldom been studied except to note their timing and sequencing relative to first births and to use them as evidence of program failure.

A neglected aspect of teenage pregnancy and parenting is micro-level research, which takes into account the perspective of the teenage mother, highlights individual diversity, and identifies coping strategies among teen mothers.

Current research, note Furstenberg, Brooks-Gunn, and Morgan fails "to take account of individual variations in outcome [which] has helped to perpetuate the negative stereotype of the teenage mother. By ignoring diversity, investigators have also missed an opportunity to understand why some young mothers manage to overcome the disadvantage associated with early childbearing while others are overwhelmed by it" (1987: 9).

As Furstenberg and his coauthors imply, it is much easier to report how teen mothers may be similar than to report on their diversity and individual ways of coping with early motherhood. This tendency may be particularly observed in research based on evaluations of programs for pregnant and parenting teens, which have been the source of much of the recent data on the subject.

Marini (1984) argues that the use of the concept of social norm is problematic in the study of the timing and sequencing of major life events. Marini proposes questions for a future research agenda: "One question is what are the micro-level *determinants* of the timing and sequencing of events marking the transition to adulthood. That is, in a sample of individuals from a given society at a particular point in time, what are the personal characteristics and life circumstances that produce variation in the process of transition to adulthood?" (Marini, 1984: 240).

Furstenberg et al. and Marini are making a case for a different kind of research on teenage pregnancy and parenting, the focus of which should be rooted in behavior and subculture customs rather than in normative life course research. An examination of micro-level aspects of coping among many individuals from the same socioeconomic and racial backgrounds may serve to correct the stereotyping of behavior among teen mothers. Further, research from the perspective of the teen mother will add a dimension of reality to the current conventional wisdom about teen pregnancy and childbearing.

Respondents were not part of a demonstration program offering comprehensive services. (See appendix A for additional background on this study). Most participants were referred by social workers in two Boston hospitals that gather data through the Massachusetts Adolescent Pregnant and Parenting System (MAPPS) on pregnant teens who have not completed high school. Demographic and health data for MAPPS are gathered at six-, twelve-, eighteen-, and twenty-four–month intervals. This data was used for choosing the sample of fifteen teens with one baby and fifteen teens with two babies.

An important feature of the study is the location of the interviews. All but four respondents were interviewed in their homes. This permitted the findings to be firmly rooted in the participants' social environment of home and neighborhood.

Design

It was my purpose to construct an interview guide that covered the respondents' perspectives on pregnancy, birth, children, and the role of significant others in relation to these topics. Virtually all students of adolescent pregnancy report that teenage girls do not plan to become pregnant. I assumed, therefore, that the respondents in this study probably did not plan their pregnancies. Unplanned pregnancies precipitate a series of crises and decision points for the expectant mother. The teenage mother's thoughts, feelings, and actions relating to these crisis events of pregnancy, pregnancy resolution, birth, and motherhood will reveal her perspective. I therefore asked questions that would permit respondents to tell me their thoughts and experiences as well as the part significant others played in influencing those experiences. The narrative responses about critical events provide the respondents' perspectives, the primary data for the study.

The interview guide (see appendix C) for this study was developed by using interview questions from other studies of pregnancy, birth, motherhood, adolescent sexual behavior, and the development of self-esteem and identity during adolescence. The Child Welfare League of America (CWLA) research center librarian provided copies of the two interview schedules designed for the CWLA study directed by Shelby H. Miller (1983), *Children as Parents: A Study of Childbearing and Child Rearing Among 12- to 15-Year-Olds*. The interview guides provided the framework and general guidelines for developing the content and format of this study.

The CWLA study was designed to elicit brief and easily coded responses to sociodemographic data. This format is useful for gathering information such as age, sex, living arrangements, mobility, income sources, work history, educational achievement, and educational aspirations. Ideas for questions about feelings related to being a mother, pregnancy, and pregnancy resolution came from the CWLA study, for example,

- Now I want you to think back to when ——— was born. How do you remember feeling and thinking about being a mother?
- Tell me what it's like being a mother now. Can you describe what it means to you?
- How did you feel when you first found out you were pregnant?
- Who was the first person you confided in as soon as you knew you were pregnant?
- How did this person react?

- How did your mother react?
- Just before you became pregnant the first time, did you want to become pregnant when you did?
- Did you consider having an abortion or giving the baby up for adoption? (see appendix C, questions 8, 9, and 62–67)

The CWLA interview included an eighteen item self-esteem questionnaire that used items from Coopersmith's Self-Esteem Inventory (1967) and Rosenberg's Self-Esteem Scale (1965). These same self-esteem questions were administered to each respondent in this study during the second half of the interview (see appendix C, questions 53-1–53-18). A series of questions on self-concept and self-identity, taken from a questionnaire developed for Matina S. Horner's study *Cognitive and Emotional Development in Early Adolescence,*[9] were intended to elicit the ways respondents think of themselves:

- Who in your family are you most like?
- What about you is similar to that person?
- Do you identify strongly, somewhat strongly, a little, or not at all with that person?
- Can you say who has been the most important (influential) person in your life? Tell me about that person.
- How would that person describe you? (see appendix C, questions 48–52)

Questions on self-esteem and self-concept were included because identity formation is the major psychological task of adolescence. How one carries out the tasks of forming a sexual identity and ideas about future roles and relationships is critical to understanding adolescent behavior. Low self-esteem is associated with school dropout and poor school performance. Adolescent mothers are often school dropouts; therefore problems with self-esteem and identity formation may be related to dropping out of school and having babies.

In this study, the structured self-esteem questionnaire was viewed as one way of exploring how respondents feel about themselves. Other questions were included that allowed respondents to describe persons and events that affect how they evaluate themselves. For example, respondents were asked to talk about events that had made them feel good about themselves and to describe the most important people in their lives. A "description in which an important figure in a person's life history serves as an exemplar of some particular ideal in action" is known as idealization, one of the constructs that aids in the understanding of self-esteem (Jackson, 1984: 40).

Questions on decision making were included to elicit information about the teen mother's role in the household, her autonomy, and how she and the adults in the house shared decision making, especially in relation to the children. Questions 59 and 60 (see appendix C) were taken from a *Draft Interview for Mothers and Grandmothers* developed by Deborah Kline Walker at the Harvard School of Public Health:[10]

- Who makes most of the decisions in your family?
- How do you fit into the decision-making process? For example, if your child(ren) had pretty bad colds and you had to go out, who would decide whether you should go?

A survey by Robert Coles and Geoffrey Stokes (1985), *Sex and the American Teenager*, served as a guide in wording new questions.

Data Collection

I began interviewing in May 1987. Between May and November, I completed fifteen interviews with mothers of two babies. Between November 1987 and March 1988, I completed fifteen interviews with mothers of one child. Each interview took approximately four hours, including travel and interview time.

The Interview Setting

Twenty-six interviews were conducted in respondents' homes. Interviews usually took place in the living room or at the kitchen table. Two mothers preferred to be interviewed in their bedrooms, which they shared with their children. Three interviews were conducted at community health centers. One interview was conducted in the hospital a day after the respondent gave birth to her second child.

I preferred seeing the mothers at home because I could gather data through observations about neighborhoods, housing conditions, and the interactions between family members, study participants, and others present in the household. The disadvantages of home interviews were the distractions caused by television sets, telephones, doorbells, crying babies, and so on. I regarded the presence of the children as a positive distraction because it provided me the opportunity to observe their development and interaction with their mothers.

The Interview Process

At the beginning of the interview, respondents were asked what they knew about the study. Most had a vague idea based on a conversation with the social worker who had informed them about it. The positive regard respondents had for social workers at Brigham and Women's and St. Margaret's hospitals clearly benefited my research. Respondents linked their social workers to the birth event and the caring they had received during the prenatal period. Several of the respondents had attended school at St. Mary's Home, which is part of St. Margaret's, during the second half of their pregnancy. For some mothers, St. Mary's had been their first positive school experience. Thus that these young mothers linked my research to their social workers greatly increased trust and probably raised the response rate.

I identified myself as a student doing research for a dissertation about what it is like to be a teenage mother. I described the study as different from other studies because it would focus on what young mothers think rather than on what others think. Respondents were given the opportunity to ask questions about the study, we then read the consent form (see appendix B) together. When the purpose of the interview was clear, I asked for permission to record our conversation. All of the mothers allowed the interviews to be recorded and interviews lasted between one and one-quarter and two and one-half hours.

The tape recorder permitted me to listen rather than write. When children were present, they could be counted on to be curious about the tape recorder. Mothers usually reacted by trying to keep children from touching the recorder. I handled this by inviting children to talk into the recorder and listen to their voices before the formal interview began. This put respondents at ease, satisfied the children's curiosity, and provided an opportunity to test the recording equipment. After this initial focus on the recorder, it seemed to be forgotten and did not interfere with free expression.

The interview schedule is structured but the questions were administered in an open-ended way. During the pretest interviews, it became clear that it is advisable to write as little as possible during the interview. The mothers talked more openly when given undivided attention. Thus, only short factual responses such as dates and ages, as well as responses to the self-esteem and attitude and belief questions, were written. The rest of the structured interview schedule was used as a guide for making sure that all content areas were covered. In sum, the structured questionnaire was used as an interview guide rather than a set of sequential questions. The highly structured format of the interview guide was most useful in the human subjects review process. While I abandoned using it as a sequential set of questions, the process of preparing the questions helped me to follow responses with probes and kept me from missing areas I wanted to cover with each mother.

Some respondents told their life story without much prodding. Others were less responsive, especially to open-ended questions. Respondents varied widely in verbal ability and capacity for abstract thinking. Some gave concrete responses to abstract questions. For example, the question "Does the picture you have of yourself in the future satisfy you?" sometimes elicited an answer regarding a photograph. In such instances, questions were rephrased to make the meaning clear. I learned with each interview and revised my approach in subsequent interviews. For example, in the first interviews, the self-esteem questions were asked midway through the interview. I discovered that these questions could disrupt a free-flowing conversation and influence respondents' answers to later questions. Therefore, in subsequent interviews, I asked the self-esteem questions near the end of the interview.

Most of the women welcomed an opportunity to talk about their lives. They were responsive to my interest in understanding what it means to be a mother from the perspective of a teenager. The

value they placed on education made them identify positively with
my role as a student.

Themes

With thirty completed interviews, all on tape, I followed a procedure to identify and classify the major themes in the interviews. The
first step was listening to each tape-recorded interview and making
notes about it. Each interview was heard as soon as possible after it
was conducted out of sheer interest and excitement. Because my
written record of the interview was almost completely confined to
demographic data and responses to the self-esteem scale, the tapes
became the dependable record of the data gathered until the interviews were transcribed. In retrospect, I realize that the immediate
reliving of the interview through listening and reviewing notes fixed
each respondent and her life story in my memory. These memories
about the meaning of events from the respondents' perspectives
helped me to identify common themes and became important build-
ing blocks for an in-depth analysis of the data. The second step
consisted of reading the notes I made after the interview with observations about the respondent, the child(ren), interactions between
family members, nonverbal cues, and the neighborhood.

The third step was making a transcript of the interviews, which
I then reviewed for accuracy and thoroughness. The creation of a
verbatim record of each interview turned out to be expensive but
was necessary and valuable, as qualitative researchers have suggested (Schneider and Conrad, 1983; Mishler, 1986). Originally it
was my intent to transcribe the interviews myself; however, after
transcribing three, I realized how time-consuming this would be and
hired a transcriber. Some transcripts filled seventy pages, and others
were only half as long. I read each completed transcript while listening to the corresponding tape and repeated this process several times
for portions of each interview. By repeatedly hearing and reading
each young mother's story, I began to identify themes and to recognize how respondents retold events related to pregnancy and birth
and how they viewed their current circumstances.

The story was the universal mode respondents used to make
meaning of their lives for themselves and for others (Bruner, 1986b;

Mishler, 1986). From the systematic analysis of themes in respondents' narratives, explanations emerged that helped me to understand behavior leading to black teenage childbearing. I found that hypotheses took shape as I reread the respondents' life stories and systematically wrote memos and coded themes.

Memos covered a range of ideas and questions. For example, observations about ways that mothers responded to the demands of children during the interview, or the repetition of themes such as responsibility, were developed in memos that varied in length from two or three paragraphs to five or six pages. I coded themes by making notations with different colored pencils in the margins of the interview guide. This was the primary mode of data analysis for developing a "grounded theory" in this study, as recommended by Glaser and Strauss (1967).

Another element central to my approach was the recognition that narrative is a vehicle for a girl's expression of how she understands her life and her culture. In the words of Bruner:

> the construction of the narrative of one's own life is deeply affected by the narrative forms made available to the human imagination by a culture. For the tool kit of any culture is replete not so much with a stock of model life narratives, but of combinable constituents from which life stories can be constructed: scenarios and stances, heroes and villains, actors and protagonists, genres and types, and the rest. For a culture, if it is anything, is a jigsaw set of instructions about possible and permissible ways of constructing a "life." (Bruner, 1986b: 2, 3)

Narrative statements were analyzed to identify themes that would aid in the understanding of each respondent's interpretation of the "set of instructions" she received from her culture. Bruner (1986b: 6) defines *theme* as the timeless aspect of a story, "the transcendent plight that a story is about." He gives as examples thwarted ambitions and other universally experienced plights. Unintended pregnancy, which leads to premature motherhood, is itself such a theme in the human experience.

Narrative analysis requires sensitivity to speech patterns and to how language is used to deal with reality. Sophisticated linguistic analysis is beyond the scope of this study, but attention was given to the way in which respondents' spoke about emotionally laden events (Bruner, 1986b). Such events are often handled by speaking about past events or relationships as if they were part of present experience. This was vividly illustrated when one respondent was asked the following:

Interviewer: Tell me something about your father.
Respondent: Well, my father—I did not grow up with my father. *But at times I get to see my father whenever I want* [emphasis added]. I wish now he could get to see his granddaughter because he hasn't seen her yet.

The respondent had last seen her father when she was pregnant. She does not know where he lives, though she reported that he is in Boston. As this story unfolded, it became difficult to distinguish between fantasy and fact. The respondent's mother and father had not married, and her father had never lived with the family. Given these circumstances, it is likely that the respondent wishes she could see her father whenever she desires, but that this is unlikely to occur. One would miss the complex mixture of meaning and longing if such discourse were considered simply a set of factual or nonfactual statements.

To understand the meaning of the experience of having children from the respondents' perspectives, I chose to analyze the dominant themes that emerged from the interviews: the initial reaction to pregnancy, unintended pregnancies but wanted births, responsibility, and self-esteem.

The exploration of the respondent's reaction to pregnancy and the reaction of the persons she chose to tell was a means of discovering how pregnancy was regarded by the teenager and the significant people in her life. I expected to find a wide range of reactions and ways of coping with an event that is known to evoke ambivalence. It is during the weeks following the discovery of pregnancy that decisions are made about pregnancy resolution. The respondents already knew the outcome of their pregnancy, but what they didn't know was what was involved in the decision to have a baby and keep it. Even if pregnancy is unintended and "just happens," the teenager and those in whom she confides have the opportunity to weigh the pros and cons of having a baby or having an abortion, of getting married or becoming a single mother.

Whether or not a woman chooses to have an abortion or to marry before the baby is born according to Zelnik, Kanter, and Ford, is related to pregnancy intention among white and middle-class young women (1981). If the pregnancy was unintended, abortion is likely to occur. If pregnancy was intended, the chances are high that the woman will marry before the birth. This, however is not true for young black women. Even when pregnancy is unintended, black women are more likely to have the baby and remain unmarried.

The psychological need for independence, love, and acceptance are common human needs. For adolescents, these needs are critical to the development of identity and self-worth. Seeking love and acceptance through sexual involvement and expressing the need to care and be cared for by others through having a baby are costly ways, however, of working out the high value females place on caring (Gilligan, 1982). Taking risks and acting irresponsibly while being pulled toward responsibility are natural tensions inherent in moving from adolescence to adulthood. Finding the solution to these tensions requires cognitive skills and moral judgments beyond the capabilities of many teenagers. Moral development is dependent on such cognitive skills as perception of reality and evaluation of experiences (Muuss, 1982). Further, moral judgments are based upon one's life experiences (Muuss, 1982).

Low self-esteem and poor self-concept are psychological constructs often associated with teenagers who become pregnant. In the past these constructs were viewed as individual problems rather than results of cumulative experiences in the family and social institutions.

In the self-esteem questionnaire that I administered to each respondent, the responses were scored on a four-point scale with 4 assigned to "agree strongly" and 1 assigned to "disagree strongly" for items that represent a positive direction. For items representing a negative direction, 1 was the value assigned to "agree strongly" and 4 to "disagree strongly." The sum of the scores on the eighteen items represents the respondent's self-esteem score. The scores were arranged from the lowest to highest and were correlated with the following variables: number of babies, education, presence or absence of support from father, age at first birth, and age at interview.

The findings in chapter 5 focus on the role of primary socialization in the careers of teen mothers. The descriptive demographic data that follows, such as age at first birth, age at interview, living arrangements, educational status, employment status, the age at which respondents' mothers began childbearing, and income sources, provide a context for the teenage mothers' responses.

The Sample

The mothers were in the range of sixteen to twenty years of age at the time they were interviewed. When they gave birth to their first child they were between fifteen and eighteen years old. Over a third, or twelve of the mothers, gave birth to their first child at seventeen.

For mothers of two children, the mean age at the birth of their first child was 16.2. Similarly, for mothers of one child, the mean age at their first birth was 16.3 (see Table 4–1). This lack of difference suggests that factors other than age are associated with second births. Education may be a key factor. For example, girls who did not have a second baby more often returned to school after the birth of the first baby, whereas those with second babies did not.

The educational level of the sample reveals that eleven of the thirty mothers had less than a high school education. Of these eleven

Table 4–1
Age of Respondent at First Birth

	Mothers of Two Children	Mothers of One Child	Total
Fifteen	4	5	9
Sixteen	5	2	7
Seventeen	5	7	12
Eighteen	1	1	2
Total	15	15	30
Mean age	16.2	16.3	16.2

Table 4–2
Educational Status by Number of Children

| | Number of Children | | |
	Two	One	Total
Less than twelfth grade	9	2	11
Enrolled in high school	1	5	6
Enrolled in equivalency	0	3	3
High school graduate	2	1	3
Post–high school program	3	2	5
Enrolled in college	0	2	2
Total	15	15	30

high school dropouts, nine had two children. These nine respondents averaged 17.4 months between first and second births, whereas those who graduated from high school averaged 23.4 months between the births of the first and the second child. In comparison, only two respondents with one child are dropouts, and eight with one child were enrolled in high school or equivalency programs at the time they were interviewed. None of the respondents with two children are in college, but two of the mothers with one child are enrolled in college, and three respondents with two children are attending post–high school training programs (see Table 4–2). The educational achievement among these mothers is consistent with previous research findings that repeat births are

Table 4–3
Living Arrangements of Respondents and Their Children

Living Arrangements	Mothers of Two Children	Mothers of One Child	Total
Respondents' mother	11	9	20
Father of child(ren)	0	3	3
Boyfriend	1	1	2
Relative	3	1	4
Respondent and child(ren) only	0	1	1
Total	15	15	30

Table 4–4
Income Sources of Mothers with Two Children

	AFDC	Respondent's Job	Respondent's Mother's Job	Respondent's Father's Job	Children's Father's Job	Other Relatives' Job	Other Government Source
Agnes	X				X		
Beth	X				X		SSI (grandmother)
Natalie	X						
Corrie	X		X				
Sandy[a]	X						
Mae	X				X		
Grace	X[b]		X		X		
Joyce		X			X		foster care (mother)
Kate	X[b]		X		X	X	
Penny	X		X		X	X	
Liz	X					X	
Dee			X	X[c]		X	
Tracy	X						
Krista		X	X	X	X		
Virginia	X						
Total	12	2	6	2	8	4	2

[a]Sandy lives with a man who is father to neither of her children. He is employed full-time and shares household expenses.
[b]Children get AFDC but mother doesn't.
[c]Respondent's father pays child support.

Table 4–5
Income Sources of Mothers with One Child

	AFDC	Respondent's Job	Respondent's Mother's Job	Respondent's Father's Job	Children's Father's Job	Other Relatives' Job	Other Government Source
Cher	X		X		X[c]		
Annie			X				Survivors' Benefit
Jackie	X						
Ivy	X	X (20 hrs.)	X		X		
Robbie	X		X				
Nellie	X[b]		X	X	X		
Peggy	X				X		
Linda	X						
Margie	X		X			X	
Arlene[a]	X						
Robin		X					
Loretta	X[b]		X	X	X[c]		
Emma	X		X				
Hattie		X			X		
Shelly		X					
Total	11	4	8	2	6	1	1

[a]Arlene lives with a man who is not the father of her child. He is employed full-time and shares household expenses.
[b]Child gets AFDC but mother doesn't.
[c]Children's father pays child support.

likely to interfere with school completion; and mothers who have
rapid repeat pregnancies (that is, pregnancies within two years of a
first birth) are more likely not to return to school after the birth of
the first baby.

Twenty of the thirty respondents live with their mothers (the
majority of whom were unmarried). Eleven of the respondents are
mothers of two children and nine have one child. Three respondents
with one child live with the father of the child, whereas no respondents with two children live with the father of the children. One
mother in each group lives with a boyfriend who is not the father of
the child(ren). Three respondents with two children live with a
relative, as compared with one mother of one child. Only one
respondent in the sample lives alone with her child (see Table 4–3).

Twenty-three of these young mothers reported AFDC as a
source of income. Of the twenty-three, four reported receiving aid
for only the children. Fourteen respondents reported their mothers'
job as a source of income. Five respondents reported working full-
time, and one respondent works half-time. Fourteen of the respon-

Table 4–6
Respondents with Two Children

	Age at First Birth	Age at Second Birth	Age at Interview	Mother Was a Teen Mother[a]
Agnes	17	18	18	Yes (18)
Beth	15	17	17	Yes (18)
Natalie	17	18	19	Yes (18)
Corrie	16	18	19	Yes (16)
Sandy	16	18	19	Yes (15)
Mae	16	17	18	Yes (17)
Grace	15	17	17	No
Joyce	18	20	20	Yes (18)
Kate	15	16	16	Yes (16)
Penny	17	19	19	Yes (12)
Liz	16	19	20	No
Dee	16	17	17	Yes (14)
Tracy	17	19	19	Yes (17)
Krista	17	19	19	No
Virginia	15	16	16	Yes (17)

Table 4–7
Respondents with One Child

Respondent	Age at First Birth	Age at Interview	Mother Was Teen Mother
Cher	17	19	No
Annie	15	18	Yes (16)
Jackie	17	19	Yes (16)
Ivy	17	19	NA
Robbie	16	19	No
Nellie	16	18	Yes (17)
Peggy	18	20	Yes (14 or 15)
Linda	17	19	Yes (17)
Margie	15	17	Yes (14)
Arlene	17	20	No
Robin	15	18	Yes (19)
Loretta	15	17	No
Emma	17	19	Yes (18)
Hattie	17	20	Yes (18)
Shelly	15	16	Yes (14 or 15)

dents reported receiving some financial help from the father of their child(ren). Only two fathers, each with one child, made formal child support payments. Thus, most of the fathers' financial contributions cannot be depended on as a regular source of support. Two respondents live with employed men who are not fathers of their children but who share household expenses with them.

While over two-thirds of the respondents receive AFDC, half the mothers of respondents and half the fathers of the children make financial contributions to the young mothers and their children. Thus, it may be more accurate to think of the majority of respondents as engaging in "income packaging," that is, putting together income from welfare and a number of other sources, rather than as being welfare dependent (see Tables 4–4 and 4–5).

Tables 4–6 and 4–7 present the names (actual names are not used to protect the privacy of respondents) of women in the interview sample and identify them by age at first birth, age at interview, and age at which their mothers began childbearing.

5
Socialized to Motherhood

What are the advantages of being a mother so young? Umm, well, when I was twelve my sister had a baby, so I helped her take care of it. So I was already in the knowledge of taking care of a baby. I think she was sixteen when she had her first baby. My mother had prepared us for motherhood, so everything was fine.

—Arlene, a mother at seventeen

This chapter focuses on the primary socialization of respondents, the process that prepares persons to fit into their social environment by assuming roles defined as age-appropriate and that occurs largely within the family. The example of adult family members is a key aspect in the preparation of children to assume the roles of worker and parent. Data presented here suggest that teenage pregnancy and childbearing are partly explainable in terms of the process of socialization in the family.

The socialization explanation for patterns of reproductive behavior in families is supported by several researchers (Marini, 1984; Hogan and Kitagawa, 1985; McLanahan and Bumpass, 1988). Marini examines the concept of socialization for a possible explanation of behavior or its consequences in the transition from adolescence to adulthood. She suggests that "preferences for the timing and sequencing of role changes are products of socialization, arising from internalization of the predominant behavior patterns of significant others" (1984: 232). Hogan and Kitagawa along with McLanahan and Bumpass emphasize two aspects of socialization: parental role models and parental supervision.

Adolescence is a time when educational and vocational aspirations are set and personal goals for the future are identified. Family, peers, ethnic group, school, and other neighborhood institutions shape the teenager's ideas about the self and the future. Parental role models partly determine what the adolescent accepts as a possible life course. For respondents in this study, the adolescent struggle with "becoming" an adult is preempted by early motherhood and its accompanying responsibilities. Although the respondents report that their pregnancies were accidental, an examination of family influences reveals that the foundation for the occurrence of motherhood was established long before adolescence.

Mothers and Daughters

Becoming a mother during adolescence represents the repetition of a familiar cultural pattern. Instructions received by these young mothers about ways of constructing life are embedded in the cultural context of black inner-city families. The predominant pattern of family life familiar to the respondents was the single-parent household headed by a mother who began childbearing when she was a teenager. Most of the mothers of respondents had children by more than one man but had never married. Early childbearing outside of marriage was common in their families and neighborhoods. Teenage girls were aware of their mother's childbearing history, which typically began before the age of nineteen and prior to marriage.

Seventy-three percent of the thirty respondents were daughters of women who had begun childbearing when they were teenagers. Of this 73 percent, 16.6 percent of respondents' mothers had been young teens (twelve to fifteen) when their first child was born. Less than a third of all of the respondents reported that their mothers delayed childbearing until age twenty or older. Thirty percent had sisters who were teen mothers. In addition, respondents had cousins who were teen mothers as well as unmarried aunts in their twenties and thirties who had young children. Even respondents who do not spend their early years with their mothers, as teenagers may be at risk for early childbearing in an environment filled with childbearing female role models. For example, Natalie, nineteen, had been reared by her grandmother in a rural southern town until she was sixteen, at which age she had come to Boston to live with her mother, who had been 18 and unmarried when Natalie was born.

During her three years in Boston, Natalie had two children. Ten people, including Natalie and her children, lived in her mother's apartment. In addition to Natalie's sons, a year and one-half and six months old, her sister, seventeen, had an eight-month-old baby and her twenty-eight-year-old unmarried aunt had a one-year-old child. Adolescent socialization and multiple family role models of single parents are powerful influences on family formation behavior (McLanahan and Bumpass, 1988).

The majority of respondents had lived most of their lives in female-headed households. Most (66.6 percent) still lived with their mothers and were thereby subfamilies in female-headed households. Only 26.6 percent of the mothers of respondents had married but not all had married the fathers of the respondents. Three respondents, Cher, Loretta, and Krista, had grown up in two-parent households; however, Cher's father had died when she was seventeen, and Loretta's mother and father had separated when she was fifteen. Krista's parents, who had been married for over twenty-five years, were the only set of married parents still living together among the thirty teenage mothers, and their daughter, Krista, was the only respondent of the thirty who was married. But at the time she was interviewed, Krista was separated from her husband and living with her parents.

The mothers of most respondents were in their late thirties. Some of them had children close in age to their daughter's child(ren). For example, Nellie's baby was fourteen months old, and her thirty-five-year-old mother, recently remarried, had a two-year-old son. Others, like Tracy, had a child three years old, the same age as her mother's youngest child. Thus, as Bruner suggests, narratives of ones own life and the available life stories of other persons provide instructions about "permissible ways of constructing a life" (1986b).

A scarcity of role models in their immediate environment who exercised other life options suggested to respondents that having children while young and unmarried is acceptable and perhaps expected behavior, yet nearly half of the respondents also had working mothers as role models, some of whom had completed high school requirements later in life. Respondents with working mothers often expressed interest in the same or an occupation similar to that of their mothers. For example, several respondents whose mothers were in health professions aspired to be nurses, and one respondent wanted to be a beautician like her mother, who owned her own shop. Surprisingly, however, respondents did not identify with teachers or other professional or semiprofessional women they had met. Respondents identified their mother as the most influential and helpful person in their lives. Only one respondent named two professional women outside of her family and neighborhood as role models. Not one respondent mentioned a teacher, which was surprising given the number of hours spent in school, even if one drops out.

Supervision

In addition to having several siblings, some respondents had had to care for younger children because their mothers worked. Other respondents may not have had childcare responsibilities but had been left unsupervised for long periods of time. The absence of supervised activities leaves children who have already been exposed to role models involved in early childbearing and unmarried parenthood vulnerable to early sexual involvement (Hogan and Kitagawa, 1985).

The symptoms of growing up in families and neighborhoods that offer few supervised activities to latency-age children were reflected in the lives of several young mothers in this study. Middle childhood or latency usually does not have as its focus sexual identity but rather the establishment of industry, competence, and the avoidance of inferiority (Erikson, 1968). In this stage of development, children begin to assume new and more responsible roles, which are rewarded by approval and a sense of mastery. This development cannot occur without instruction and supervision from adults. Children in families where the father is absent begin with diminished possibilities of receiving supervision simply because one parent cannot do the work of two. Matters may be worsened if the mother works long hours. Childcare for children of working mothers is a national issue that cuts across class and race, but middle-class families and suburban single, working mothers who are not available after school to provide instruction and supervision often depend on extended school activities and neighborhood institutions for recreational programs. Such activities were missing from the lives of my respondents.

The young women in my sample often replaced extracurricular activities and sports with early sexual exploration and behavior designed to get the attention of parents. For example, some girls had run away repeatedly or left home altogether with the hope that a working mother or a mother preoccupied with her own relationships would take notice. Respondents in my study missed the parental and institutional support in the preteen years necessary to establish the sense of self that comes from performing rewarding tasks and getting feedback from significant adults. They did not receive adequate instruction about bodily changes, relationships with males, and the consequences of sexual activity. Missing supervision and poor parental relationships contributed to early sexual activity and pregnancy. Sandy's story illustrates what can happen when a preadolescent daughter's care becomes secondary to other priorities in her mother's life and no substitute care is provided.

Sandy, nineteen, is the mother of a three-year-old son and a ten-month-old daughter. She lives north of Boston in a spacious subsidized apartment, which she shares with a man who is not the father of either of her children. Sandy was pleased to tell her story. She could hardly believe what she had accomplished in the past five years of her life. She had received her high school equivalency before her first child was born. At the time of the interview, Sandy was scheduled to enter an office management training course. She said, "I love my life now." This, however, had not always been the case. Sandy had been neglected by her mother, who became involved with a drug addict when Sandy was nine years old. Sandy's mother had not noticed Sandy's sexual activity, which had begun when she was eleven with "the kid next door," the son of her mother's best friend. At twelve, Sandy had begun running away; she tripped on acid at fourteen; and by age fifteen she lied about her age to get a job as a salesclerk. Sandy had seen herself as the center of her mother's life until Mark, a cocaine addict, became her mother's companion. Her mother's relationship with Mark had lasted throughout Sandy's teenage years.

So what happened was he started taking my mother away from me. He had another apartment in the city and he would take her for three or four days at a time, and she would go. She was just as responsible as he was because she was not thinking, *"I have a nine-year-old daughter at home." And maybe if she had been there when she was doing all this running around, maybe if she had been there for me, I wouldn't have resorted to the street. Negative attention is better than none.* I didn't have her, so I went to my friends. And she never came to me so I just automatically made up my mind that she didn't care about me any more.

In retrospect, Sandy regards her mother as a victim of family circumstances. When Sandy's mother was fifteen, she and her siblings witnessed the murder of their mother by their father. Shortly after the shooting, Sandy's mother became pregnant with Sandy's sister, who is eight years older than Sandy. Sandy's mother left this child in the South and moved to Boston where Sandy was born. She had worked as a dancer in the combat zone. Sandy thinks that she and her mother have been through some "amazing stuff." She evaluates her life as more positive than her mother's, and she feels that she thinks more clearly at nineteen than her mother does at forty-three.

Because of the necessity of work other mothers had not been at home to supervise their daughters. The hours between the end of school and the time a mother comes home from work are left to the child to fill. It was during this time that Ivy had turned to an older crowd and to boys. Being alone after school and at night while her mother, who was separated from Ivy's father, was pursuing her social life had allowed Ivy to have long hours alone with her boyfriend.

Ivy, a mother at seventeen, described herself as a "beebopper" in her earlier years. "I used to be running around and stuff. I wanted to be a swinger when I was twelve, eleven years old. About thirteen, I tried to be with the older kids and stuff. That's when I had my first boyfriend." Ivy became sexually active at fifteen. Sexual activity was a substitute for the closeness missing in her family. Without activities or adult supervision after school, Ivy turned to her boyfriend.

He was someone to lean on. When I was depressed, I figured, I'll lean on him. Next thing you know, I figure I started to listen to him. Then I saw him as more of a friend. Then why not kiss him? Why not touch him? It seemed that one thing led to another. Afterwards we never made a big deal out of it like "wow, wasn't that great last night." We never even talked much about it. It was like, that was a nice night. That was nice, but don't talk about it. We said we shouldn't have let it happen, it won't happen again. And then it did happen again. My mom didn't get home 'til after six. *I was home by myself from about two-o'clock.* He'd just come by, then he'd go home and tell his mom he just came from school. Then he'd come by my house again around seven-thirty. My mother thought, "What a nice guy, he comes by the house to do homework." She never knew. *My mom went out partying around eleven* PM *and he'd go home around one or two in the morning before she got home. You know every teenager has a scam—how to have things regulated in the house. How to get over with moms and dads and everything.*

For Ivy, seeking love and responsiveness in the context of no parental supervision led to sexual activity and pregnancy. Her own evaluation that "we shouldn't have let it happen" indicates that the presence of adults or activities might have set limits that Ivy could not have set for herself.

Similarly, Nellie's mother worked and Nellie reports that she would come straight home from the suburban school she attended. She did not have neighborhood friends because she was going to school out of the neighborhood, but she had a steady boyfriend who always came to her house. They drifted into sexual activity and she became pregnant at sixteen. She reports that her mother "wasn't strict." Ivy and Nellie had mothers who worked full-time and made efforts to see that decent schooling was provided, but who seemed unaware that without supervision they might "drift" into sexual activity. Other respondents' behavior patterns were not of the benign type that simply drift into sexual activity. Poor parental relationships and behavior that one might predict would end in pregnancy are illustrated by Kate.

Kate describes herself as a rebellious teen who ran away from home at thirteen to escape her mother's supervision. She had stayed away from home for two years during which time she lived a few blocks away from her mother with a woman who worked in the combat zone. She reports that her mother had not known where she was but that she had occasionally visited her grandmother who also lived in the neighborhood. Kate had no contact with her mother until she was fifteen years old and pregnant. At the time she was interviewed, just before her seventeenth birthday, Kate was the mother of an infant and a seventeen-month-old daughter.

When Kate's first pregnancy was confirmed, she decided it was time to go home. She asked her mother to sign papers so that she could get an abortion. An argument followed, and the papers were not signed. Kate returned to her grandmother's house. In a few days Kate's mother called her and asked her to come home because "at this point you need a mother to talk to." Kate links her pregnancies to her poor relationship with her mother. When I asked her to tell me what happened and whether or not she used birth control, she replied:

> No. Me and my mother, we didn't have a close relationship. You know because I would run away, we didn't have a close relationship then. And, I don't know, I think maybe if we was a little closer and she would talk to me, and everything—I always tell her this too. I always say, you know, I'm not blaming nothing on you or anything, but maybe if we had a close relationship, and I could come to you and talk to you about things, things would be different now. Everything would be okay. Maybe I wouldn't have Vera and Yvonne. Everything would be different. Well, as we were growing up, I was a brat, okay? At that time I got into everything; I did everything; I talked back. But, I don't know, maybe.... I don't know where things went wrong. And maybe it's because she was harder on my two sisters. Maybe if she was harder on me, things would be better.

Kate's reflection on her situation reveals the perspective that her relationship with her mother and the lack of discipline and supervision had more to do with her pregnancies than the availability of birth control. She thinks that the reason her twenty-two- and twenty-one-year-old sisters did not get pregnant was because her mother was "real hard on them." Pregnancy not only brought her back home but put her under her mother's supervision, which in spite of her rebellion, Kate felt she needed. She reported that she has a better relationship with her mother since the children were born and that her mother helps her make major decisions regarding the children.

Supervision is one way parents provide protection for children. The combined effects of single-parent status, full-time work, fractured relationships, and the absence of after-school and neighborhood activities made these parents unable to give the supervision necessary to protect their daughters from early sexual activity and subsequent pregnancy. All respondents reported that pregnancy was unintended but most did not seek to terminate the pregnancy.

Discovery and Resolution

These young mothers often resolved the question of carrying their pregnancies to term with feelings of ambivalence and in the midst of conflicting advice from parents and boyfriends. Although the respondents reported that their pregnancies had been unintended, they wanted the baby. Of the thirty mothers, only Kate, who became pregnant at fifteen, reported that her children were unwanted. She intended to abort her first pregnancy, but her mother was unwilling to give consent. She considered abortion again during her second pregnancy, but she waited until it was no longer medically safe (after 24 weeks) and was unable to have an abortion performed. She then explored giving up the second baby for foster care or adoption but was unable to make a firm decision. The most significant people in Kate's life—her mother, the baby's father, and his mother— encouraged her to keep the baby.

Respondents' and their mothers' reactions to pregnancy cover a wide range of responses. Acceptance, depression, disappointment, fear, and happiness were among the reported responses. The reactions of mothers of respondents were reported as "just getting around bragging," or "she wasn't mad, she was understanding," or "she wanted me to get an abortion because I wasn't old enough." Some boyfriends fled, and others were happy, supportive, or uninvolved. This broad range of reactions illustrates feelings universally experienced in times of crises. Ambivalence, disappointment, denial, and acceptance might be found among any group of women and men confronting an unintended pregnancy. The following examples illustrate how after a variety of initial reactions respondents reached pregnancy resolution. Arlene, whose words open this chapter, became pregnant at seventeen. She had a matter-of-fact reaction to learning that she was pregnant, which she attributes to the way her family handled the pregnancy of her sister: "My first thought was, 'I got to go tell Eric' [the father]. Okay? There was no excitement, no confusion, no nothing. Really, it was like I'm pregnant. Okay. I've got to deal with it. So I didn't have any problem with it. You know, abortion never came into my mind, 'cause I don't believe in it. So there wasn't any problem with it when I found out."

One of Arlene's sisters had had a baby at sixteen. Arlene reported that even though her mother had threatened to put out any of the girls who became pregnant, once it had happened, her sister and her baby had been welcomed by the family. Arlene's mother had died of a heart condition when Arlene was fifteen, a year before she became pregnant. After her mother's death, she had lived with her father and his girlfriend, who were supportive during the pregnancy and after the child was born.

Arlene's greatest shock was her boyfriend's reaction to her pregnancy. Shortly after she told him she was pregnant, he left town and went South to live with relatives. At the time she was interviewed, Arlene was a sophomore in college living with a businessman to whom she was engaged. Arlene's experience with her father, who had never married her mother but had stuck by Arlene even after her mother died, may have left her unprepared for being deserted by the baby's father. At the same time, her father's constancy, and the fact that he is the biological father of only two of her siblings but had acted as a father to all four siblings, may have influenced her to establish a new relationship with a man she plans to marry.

Nearly half of the respondents' boyfriends were pleased about the pregnancy and remain emotionally involved and financially supportive, as does the father of Nellie's baby. The first person Nellie told when she became pregnant at sixteen was her boyfriend. He was pleased. He and his family provide financial support and take the baby for weekend visits. Of her mother's reaction, Nellie explained, "At first, she didn't seem like she was so upset. Then after a while, she talked to me for two whole weeks straight telling me it was not going to be easy. Then it seemed like she was happy."

Nellie and her fourteen-month-old daughter live with her mother, fourteen-year-old sister, two-year-old half-brother, and stepfather. Her mother's lack of alarm about her pregnancy may have been related to her not attempting to supervise Nellie even though she knew she had a steady boyfriend who visited her almost daily. Babies and young children seemed to create interest and excitement in this family. I was waiting to interview Nellie when she came home with her daughter from her General Equivalency Diploma (GED) program. After gently chiding Nellie for keeping me waiting, Nellie's mother greeted her granddaughter with hugs and kisses and immediately took her upstairs so I could talk to Nellie. Nellie, in the course of the interview, reported that she had learned a lot about children by caring for her two-year-old brother and that her biological father, now thirty-six, had a six-month-old daughter.

Some respondents' mothers were not only accepting of pregnancy but even went so far as to treat it lightly. Peggy, one of two eighteen-year-old mothers in the sample, reported, "Well, when I told my mother, she laughed at me." I asked Peggy if she had expected her mother to be upset. Her reply was, "Well, I don't know, 'cause when my sister got pregnant, she wasn't."

Agnes, the mother of two children, became pregnant for the first time at seventeen. She was scared and disappointed. Her mother "wasn't mad; she was understanding. She asked me what was I gonna do, if I was gonna keep it or not." Of her second pregnancy, which occurred when the first baby was only four months old, Agnes said, "I didn't get rid of the first one. Why should I get rid of this one?" Some respondents' mothers took a more active role than did Agnes's mother and gave specific advice about abortion.

Liz, pregnant with her first baby at sixteen, considered an abortion, "but I had no one to sign for me and I didn't know that you can go to court and get a judge to do it behind your mother's back." Her mother advised against abortion, and Liz accepted her point of view: "I wasn't ready [to have a baby] and I thought I should wait a little longer and finish finding pleasure, but my mother didn't want that, and she made sure I kept her [Liz's daughter]. And afterwards, I said like, hey, why not? I started feeling the same, I wanted it too. It wasn't just like I had it because she wanted me to and stuff. My mother said she wants *all* her grandchildren."

I asked Liz if her mother seemed upset initially. She replied, "No, my mother wasn't upset; my mother was happy. Then when it was born, she *really* was happy. She rushed over to see me; she brought me food and stuff. She held the baby. She wanted to take the baby home." In spite of her mother's opposition to abortion, Liz reported that she had two abortions between her first and second child. When she decided to have a second baby three years after the first one, her mother "didn't say nothing. She wished it was a little boy." The second baby's father, who was not the father of her first child, wanted her to have the baby. Liz described his mother as "loving that little baby to death."

Several respondents' mothers, like Liz's mother, discouraged abortion and were pleased about becoming grandmothers. Mothers are often joined by other relatives in opposing abortion. Respondents reported that the father of the baby usually objects to abortion.

Dee, seventeen, the youngest of eleven children, had two children less than a year apart. When she became pregnant the first time, Dee considered an abortion, but her mother, father, and boyfriend opposed the idea. Dee's second pregnancy occurred because birth control pills made her asthma worse and she stopped taking them. Of her second pregnancy, Dee said, "I knew my mother wasn't gonna let me have no abortion so I said, 'I have to keep it.' I was happy. 'Cause I really wanted two boys."

These accounts indicate that for most respondents it was more acceptable to carry an unintended pregnancy to term and keep the baby than to choose abortion. Even if the teenage girl is not ready to have children, her mother and boyfriend often encourage her to have the baby. Some mothers are happy rather than ambivalent or upset about their daughter's pregnancy. Still others are anxious to achieve the status of grandmother in spite of the fact that they are not yet forty and may have young children themselves.

Other mothers react to their daughter's pregnancy by attempting to save the daughter from making a decision she may regret later. These mothers are not anxious for their daughters to go through what they have gone through. Therefore they advise their daughters to terminate the pregnancy. Jackie, seventeen, had to deal with her own ambivalence and her mother's advice to get an abortion. Jackie:

My feelings? I was at one point real happy, and on some occasions I was really down. I didn't want it. At some points I wanted to get rid of it. But I hung in there with the pregnancy and had my child. *I always wanted a baby.* My mother said to me I should get an abortion because she didn't think that my baby's father would still be there with me, because when she found out she was pregnant with me, my father wasn't there for her, and she had the experience of raising children without the fathers until her last two. My brothers' fathers were there for them when she was pregnant.

The preceding excerpts illustrate that the usual reaction of respondents and persons important to them to unintended pregnancy is to accept rather than terminate the pregnancy. Reluctance to terminate pregnancies is consistent with a culture in which many adults begin childbearing as teenagers and in which the majority of babies are born out of wedlock. Some respondents who reported that they did not intend to become pregnant were aware of the emotional needs that motivated them not to terminate pregnancies and contributed to their wanting a baby.

Unintended Pregnancies but Wanted Births

Among the reasons for wanting babies are the often cited reasons— wanting someone to love and having something to call one's own. Some respondents are able to speak in less possessive terms by speaking of the wish to take care of and nurture someone. Annie and Sandy are two respondents in touch with the deeper needs that led them to want a baby. For example, Annie reported,

I was thinking about it, but it wasn't like on purpose. My mother thought it was on purpose cause I talked about it a lot—not getting pregnant, but I talked about babies because I wanted her to have a baby so bad. I wanted to take care of somebody. Before I found out I was pregnant, I had an idea I was. There was sickness and in my head I was saying *I hope I am*. I don't know why. It was just because, if I was, it would be something I could call my own. That was somebody I can love, and I know I was real young, but I just had that feeling. I wanted someone to love, feed them, and tell them what to do, give them advice. Somebody to love; somebody to love you back. So when I found out, I wasn't surprised.

Sandy, unlike Annie, was surprised when she discovered that she was pregnant. She received the results as part of a physical exam required by the independent living program she joined when she could no longer tolerate living at home with her mother and her mother's drug-addicted lover.

> I mean I didn't even know I was pregnant when I left home. I had *no* idea. Matter of fact, how I got pregnant was sleeping with *my best friend*—this guy that lived in the building across the street. We always hung around together in high school and everything. And, uhh, we just celebrated my birthday together, *and it just happened.* It was nothing. It was a couple of days before my sixteenth birthday. He was seventeen. Then I went to the program and I'll never forget. You have to have a physical to make sure you don't have anything that you could spread throughout the house. And at my physical, that's when I found out I was pregnant. It never crossed my mind when I went to the appointment. *Never!* If anything, I thought maybe I might have a disease, maybe gonorrhea or something but I never, never, thought I was pregnant. I had never had any pregnant friends. So it was like I never experienced being around somebody who was pregnant. So then when I started showing, I started taking it in a little better. *And I actually liked the idea, because I was alone at the time, even though I was in the program. I was still alone, as far as I had no communication with my mother.*

Sandy was not consciously intending to get pregnant. The realization that she was on her own and had little hope of getting her mother's attention made having a baby an attractive prospect. During her interview, Sandy talked about finding street friends to replace her mother because she never liked being alone. A baby would be constant company and would not abandon her as her mother had.

Fathers and Daughters

A question with which I repeatedly struggled in telling the stories of my respondents is how their fathers and the fathers of their children fit into their lives. The question becomes even more complicated because my purpose is to tell a story from the respondents' perspective. Unlike the respondent's mother, her father is not obviously "on the inside" of the respondent's life. Because the father was not in the home, usually not married to the mother, and had not consistently fulfilled his economic or sociological role, it is easy to see the father as having no central place in the teenage mother's development. But the father's physical absence does not mean that he had no psychological impact on the young mother. The pattern of relationship respondents have with their fathers provides the model that some respondents seek to re-create in their relationships with men and that other respondents consciously seek to avoid. I have chosen to talk about the fathers of respondents and the fathers of respondents' children together because there is evidence that the relationships respondents had with their own fathers and respondents' experiences of their mothers' relationships with men set the stage for their attitudes toward the fathers of their children and toward marriage.

Some respondents had never known their fathers. Others knew their father's identity but had no contact with him. Still others had occasional contact, whereas some grew up with their fathers or had continuing contact with them. Of the thirty respondents, three spent all or most of their lives in a household with a father present. Of these three fathers, one is still married to and living with the respondent's mother; one separated from the family two years prior to the respondent's interview; and the third respondent's father died shortly before her child was born.

When respondents were asked to talk about their fathers, some gave the following kinds of responses:

"No comment."

"He's down South."

"That's not my friend; me and him don't get along. He likes to rule women."

"I couldn't tell you nothing about him."

"My father's an alcoholic. I used to see him laying down in the street drunk when I was a child. He loves the bottle, he don't love me."

"My mother said he's my father. When she met him she was twelve and he was in his thirties. But me and him never got along. I never considered him my father."

"I don't know nothing about him 'cause he's dead. I don't know when he died, I just know that he's dead, that's all."

Not all respondents accepted the unavailability of their fathers, nor were all of their memories negative. When I asked Jackie to tell me something about her father, she said, "Well, my father—I did not grow up with my father, *But at times I get to see my father whenever I want.* I wish now he could get to see his granddaughter because he hasn't seen her yet." Jackie last saw her father over two years ago when she was pregnant. She does not know where he lives, though she reports that he is in Boston. As Jackie told her story, it became difficult to distinguish between her wishes and actuality. Her father and mother had not married, and her father had never lived with the family. Given these circumstances, it is likely that she wishes she could see her father whenever she desires, but it is unlikely that she will see him. Jackie reveals no bitterness toward her father, only a longing to see him and have him see his grandchild. Jackie's expectations about the behavior of her child's father were clearly influenced by her experience of her father:

> When I found out I was pregnant, I thought my boyfriend was going to leave because some men or boys at that time feel that they don't want a baby. They don't want it and don't have nothing to do with it. I thought he was going to leave me when I said I was pregnant. But he stayed on with me during pregnancy and after the pregnancy. And I felt that he must really like something about me to stay on during and after the pregnancy.

In addition to not repeating the pattern established by her mother and father, Jackie has gained the kind of autonomy and control that is associated with adulthood by living with the father of her child. She values the independence and control she has gained over her life, although it means hard work. She describes life with her daughter and her daughter's father:

When I get out of school, I'm very exhausted. I have homework to do and I have to cook dinner not only for my daughter, but for my boyfriend. Because we are a family. But if you're planning to have a family, you should think about it and also try to get your boyfriend, the baby's father, to stay with you, because being a single parent will make it a lot harder on you. If I would have kept my daughter without my boyfriend, I wouldn't be living in my own home. I would be with my mother. I would be happy, but it would be difficult because my daughter is very spoiled by my mother. And I don't think I would have been able to have control over her. So with the help of my boyfriend and living out on my own—it's not easy, but it's fun.

An earlier excerpt explained that Jackie's mother had encouraged her to have an abortion because she thought Jackie's boyfriend would leave her. Jackie has succeeded in getting the father of her child to stay with her and support her, something her mother had not been able to do when Jackie was born.

Another aspect of Jackie's story illuminates matters from the young father's perspective. He was relieved when Jackie decided not to have an abortion and asked Jackie if she wanted him to live with her: "When I gave him my answer to his question, he was real happy because he has an older daughter. She's seven years old. When she was born, her mother didn't let him see his daughter." He was eighteen when he became a father the first time. He pays child support and has visitation rights. Jackie reports that she gets along well with his daughter. Jackie enjoys having his other daughter as an older sister for her daughter. Jackie is very close to her boyfriend's mother, who, she reports, was very upset that she and her son were deprived of contact with his first child.

A senior in high school when she was interviewed, Jackie thought that if she had not had a child she would be doing more to "save up for college." But to her the benefits far outweigh the delay in pursuing her educational plans: "If I wouldn't have kept my daughter, I would be missing a lot. Her love, watching her grow. I think my relationship with my boyfriend—well, we wouldn't have been together. He's so proud of his daughter. He loves her so much. He's raising a child—something he wasn't able to do with his first child."

Jackie's story illustrates the complexity of relationships between biological fathers, mothers, and their children. The absence of marriage does not erase expectations, nor does it necessarily mean that other roles will not be fulfilled by the biological father. Jackie's father rarely fulfilled his sociological or economic role—he occasionally showed up and bought Jackie "things she wanted and didn't want." She longed for him to be more involved in her life and is still searching for him. In contrast, the twenty-five-year-old father of Jackie's daughter first became a father at eighteen and was deprived of a relationship with his child. He now assumes economic responsibility for this child and has brought her into his relationship with his new family. When asked about marriage, Jackie showed me her engagement ring and said that she would marry in a year, after she had completed high school. Jackie's absent father and her boyfriend's experience of being cut off from his first child motivated the couple to establish a relationship marked by intimacy and commitment.

Liz, like Jackie, wants to know where her father is, but unlike Jackie, Liz has never met her father:

> I don't know where he's at. We used to stay with my father. My mother left from New York when I was six months old. He don't even know I got kids. And that's terrible. I tried once to contact him. My mother used to have the number of this lady they used to stay with. She called there one time, but by it being so long ago, the lady said she didn't remember my mother. She didn't know her. So she wouldn't accept the call.

Liz's mother and father never married. Liz's sixteen-year-old sister has a different father, whom her mother also did not marry. But Liz reports that her mother "used to be married, but she got a divorce." When I asked Liz about her plans to marry, she reported "that's so far off my mind, I can't even tell you that." She describes her relationship with the father of her first child as "friendly." The father of her second child, who had recently returned from the navy, visits the child and takes her to his mother's. She says that both fathers "put in time with their kids and buy them things." Liz says she gets her attitude toward men from her mother: "There are a lot of things that she does that I do. Towards men, me and her are just alike. Like as far as letting a man take advantage of us or, when it comes down to our kids, we speak for our kids first. If you don't love my kids, or if you don't like my kids, then you don't love me. We speak that way—up front, outspoken."

Liz and Jackie missed having a father, but they have chosen different ways of relating to the fathers of their children. Jackie thinks that the route of single parenthood is too difficult. She lives with the father of her daughter, is engaged to be married, and does not plan to have another child until she is married. In contrast, Liz has no plans to marry, already has two children by different fathers, and plans to have another child when her baby is a little older.

Peggy, age twenty when she was interviewed, said she hadn't known her father because her parents separated when she was seven. Her father is also the father of Peggy's twenty-four-year-old brother. Another brother, twenty-one, has a different father, and Peggy's three younger brothers have still another father. According to Peggy, her father, forty, is in the South "in the hospital because he's disabled, paralyzed. A lady shot him, that's all I know. Sometimes I talk to him on the phone." Peggy lives with the twenty-five-year-old father of her son who wants to marry her, but she's unsure that marriage will give her or her son any advantage:

> I don't know. I hope to be married, but if I'm not, it doesn't make any difference. I already got my child. And I'm in college now. I seem to be doing well, just me and him right now. Well, his father's living with me. But like I tell him, "I can take care of my son with or without him or any other man, I can take care of my son." My mother took care of seven kids by herself. She didn't have any trouble with that, so I don't think I'll have any trouble with him.

Peggy is capable of providing the necessities for her son and may not have difficulties bringing him up. She has work experience because she took computer training when she was in high school. While attending school, she had jobs that paid her $8 an hour. She plans to be an accountant when she completes college. Peggy values her independence, which is partly due to AFDC payments that give her an income and allow her to attend college. The father of Peggy's son works full-time as a security guard and has proved his commitment to her by living with her for several years. She acknowledges that he is a steady worker and a good father who spends time with their son, yet she sees no advantage to marriage.

Hattie, like Peggy, lives with the father of her son. She has never been on welfare. She works full-time in the post office and he works in an accounting firm. They share economic and child care responsibilities. Both grandmothers help with child care, which shortens the time the child spends in day care. Hattie's mother was eighteen when she married Hattie's father. They separated when Hattie was two years old but have never divorced. Hattie's father, after being out of touch for several years, now has a good relationship with Hattie and her son.

Hattie and her boyfriend have lived together almost three years. Still, she is unsure that she wants to get married:

> Sometimes I think if I would have gone into an early marriage, it probably would have broke up fast. Then, the way I look at it, I've been going with him just as long, it's like having an experience with what it would be like to be married. It's not that bad, but right now I don't want to change my name. He's asked me twice. He said, "The next time, you're gonna ask me." And it's not even the big problem about changing my name. I just don't want to go through too much. Maybe before my son gets too much older, I probably would do it. But not just to please him. Not at all. If I get married, it will be for my own benefit, that's it.

Hattie's parents did marry young, but marriage did not keep them together. It is, therefore, not surprising that Hattie is cautious about marriage. She and her boyfriend have known each other since she was fourteen. They have committed themselves to rearing their son. Clearly, economic factors are not a major hindrance to marriage since Hattie and the father of her son have secure jobs and she has never received AFDC.

Kate and Dee both still see their fathers, although their mothers and fathers never married. Kate's father lives in her neighborhood: "He comes over and everything. You know, he comes over to see the kids and to see my mother. He'll probably be over later today. He said they probably would have been together longer, but my mother's just a hard person to live with. So I believe it, I believe it 'cause you know, they argue."

Kate sees the eighteen-year-old father of her children every day. She explained,

> He gave me a ring last year while I was pregnant, I don't think I want to marry him. He talks about getting married; his mother talks about it; his father talks about it. His mother and father have been married something like twenty-five or -six years. He talks like his mother talks—she's really happy because he's the first son that's going to get married. But I'm not really thinking about it. You know, I care for him a lot, but just the three years we've been together, he's sickening. I'm tired of being around him—every time I turn around, he's there. I think it's because he's just on the next street. He's so close, when I walk out the door, he can see me. Maybe if he moved away somewhere—to another neighborhood, we would have a nice relationship. But being that I see him every day, that's why I don't think I could get married. I don't like to see a person every day. If I see you every day, I'm going to get sick of seeing your face, and I'm going to try to stay away from you, at least for a couple of weeks or something. I want to raise my kids, have a nice home, a roof over their head—all the things my mother did for us, but I want more for them. My mother always told me "Never let a man come before you and your kids."

Kate plans to have her tubes tied. She reports that she did not want to have children, but her boyfriend wanted them. Although he is just eighteen, he has graduated from high school and is a full-time construction worker. Still, Kate does not want to marry him. Unlike her boyfriend's parents, Kate's parents never married and it appears that her mother had given Kate the message that it is better to make it on your own. Kate seems unable to tolerate an intimate relationship and would be more comfortable seeing the father of her children once in a while rather than daily. Like her mother, she thinks that she and her children are a family without a father and that a father is in part an interloper between mother and child.

Dee, the youngest of eleven children, is the only child by a different father. She describes him as having eight or nine children by his current wife. He pays child support for Dee and visits her. The father of Dee's children visits every day after work. She said that she and her boyfriend "go everywhere together." Dee said she "might" get married, but "I don't want to get married, 'cause I've seen what my mother went through with her marriage and I'm not ready for that at all."

Similarly, Corrie when asked if she planned to marry, said, "No, I want to be like my mother. She's a strong independent woman, and I like my mother." Corrie's mother never married Corrie's father, who lives just up the street from them, because the two have never gotten along. Corrie does not go to visit her father because he always wants her to watch his kids. The woman he married has had three children, and he has two or three children by other women. Corrie thinks that the reason his wife has all those kids is because "she was raised to think that she was meant to serve her husband."

The father of Corrie's first son is twenty-one and the father of two other children. Corrie said she has "dropped out of contact with him. I told him don't bother me, don't mess with my son, 'cause I [have] my mother." The father does not support his child and the question of marriage has never come up, yet Corrie fears that he might try to get custody of his son. The father of her second child gives her money for both children. He is twenty. This is how she describes him:

> He's a child. He whines. He expects people to do things for him. He's nasty to me. He doesn't like to wash dishes, and he thinks I'm supposed to do them for him. He likes people to cook for him, and he irritates me. He likes to sleep and watch TV. He works down the street so I see him every day. The first time I met his father, who just moved up here, he asked, "Do you want to marry him?" I looked at him and I said, "Why would I want your son?" He said, "He might grow up after you marry him." I said, "I can't take that chance." No, I would not marry him. He acts like a baby, and I have two of my own. I don't need him plus the kids. His mother can keep him.

Corrie's view that the children belong to *her* and not also to their fathers is a sentiment often held by these young mothers. This view was supported by the respondents' mothers, who often warned against men "coming between" mother and child. For Corrie, this perspective is affirmed by her evaluation of the father of one of her children and her own ability to get employment. Corrie plans to work full-time as a typesetter. When she attended the training program, she had experience and was good enough at the trade to teach others who were having difficulty learning about the various machines. Corrie's evaluation of the immaturity and personal characteristics of her second child's father causes her to prefer her independence to marrying him.

The one married but separated respondent is hoping for a reconciliation with her husband. She attributes their breakup to his immature behavior, which she had not expected because he is five years older than she is. Krista, twenty, decided to move back to her parents' house to "teach him a lesson." He had been spending too much time with his friends and not acting responsibly. He and Krista had married before their second child was born. Krista refers to her own father as "a very wise man who sees things before they even happen. Before I got married, he had never said, "Well, Krista, that's not the thing to do." Krista's mother had urged her not to marry until her boyfriend found a place for them to live. Krista married and had lived with her husband's parents until she separated and returned to her parent's home.

Clearly, no single pattern describes the correlation between the interaction of the teenage mother and her father and her interaction with the father(s) of her child(ren). It does appear that the relationship of the respondents to their own fathers and the dynamics between the respondents' mothers and the men in their lives influence the patterns of relationship of the respondents and their children's fathers. Only six respondents reported that their parents had married. Another four mothers of respondents had married a man who was not the respondent's father. All of these marriages except one ended in divorce or separation. Two fathers of respondents who had not married the respondent's mother did assume responsibility for their daughters: one paid formal child support, and another allowed his daughter to live with him after her mother died. Two respondents lived in the same neighborhoods as their fathers and had periodic contact with them, whereas two other respondents whose parents had divorced or separated reported that their fathers had been just as influential in their lives as their mothers. Only two stepfathers were regarded as fathers by respondents.

Respondents were reluctant to make or seek long-term commitments. Staying independent like their mothers was preferred to marriage. Although the fathers of respondents' children were young (the average age of the fathers was slightly over eighteen), and those who were employed were not in high-paying jobs, at least fourteen of the thirty-six fathers (six mothers have children by two different fathers) provided some material support; two of these fourteen fathers paid formal child support. It is difficult to determine the extent of economic or material support provided by the fathers of respondents' children. Some mothers were vague about the issue of support. For example, some mothers replied, "Well, he's not working now," or "Yes, he helps out." Other fathers made cash contributions, or the paternal grandmother gave something to the baby. Some respondents mentioned that the father bought disposable diapers or clothing. Fathers who visited their children and/or still had a relationship with the mother were usually the fathers reported as providing economic assistance.

Although most of the young fathers providing some informal support to their children have low-paying jobs without much security, it is difficult to assess the influence of male employment and the low earning potential of the fathers on respondents' lack of interest in marriage. In the case of two cohabiting couples, the respondents were receiving AFDC and the fathers were working full-time. Marriage would make the mother ineligible for aid, taking away the economic independence an AFDC check gives her and decreasing total household income. One could make a better guess about the interrelationship of AFDC, jobs, and marriage after these mothers finish school and can work full-time themselves. Hattie is the best example of the possibility that male earning potential is not a factor in her reluctance to marry. She receives no welfare, and she and her son's father have stable jobs. They have also been together since high school days. Hattie's reluctance to marry is influenced by her mother and father's experience. Her parents married when they were teenagers but lived together for only a very short time. They have never divorced. Hattie remarked that getting married young is a risk. It is evident that the reasons why the few respondents who could get married do not are complex. That cohabitation is common in the society as a whole makes it an even more acceptable option for respondents.

The joblessness of black males and their lack of opportunity is viewed by Wilson (1987) as the major cause of unwed motherhood among the underclass. Joblessness and the lack of economic opportunities are certainly important factors in the marriage decisions of poor black males and females. It is possible that the availability of AFDC may contribute to the freedom of the teen mother not to marry, especially if she perceives the father of her children to be immature *and* to have limited economic prospects. But, the overwhelming socialization toward single parenthood in my respondents plays an equally important role in their attitudes toward marriage. Contrary to conventional wisdom, it is not always the teen father who is uninterested in marriage. In some cases, the father is employed (though not in the primary labor market), and he and his family are not opposed to marriage.

The majority of these thirty young unmarried mothers came from families where their own mothers had been teen mothers who in most cases never married. Some of the respondents' sisters and cousins were also teenage mothers. These reproductive patterns appear as a result of socialization, the young mother's family role models, and only casual supervision during latency and adolescence.

The absence of a father from their lives influenced many of the young mothers to think that they did not need a man to help them bring up their children. Consequently, most of the young women are not committed to marriage, though several plan to have another child.

6
Responsibility

The pregnancy was accidental. The reason I think I had the baby was to develop a sense of responsibility. I don't think it works for everyone. I would never have somebody think that it's a general rule that teenagers have babies to become more responsible, because that's not true. But it worked for me. That was what I wanted it to do, and it's done that. And now I'm responsible. And my kids are fine, and I'm fine.
—Sandy, nineteen, mother of two

I found that the young women in my study, like those studied by Ladner (1972), had been seeking to achieve independence and responsibility by becoming mothers. In this case responsibility involves the fulfillment of duties inherent in the role of mother and the capability of choosing between right and wrong. At a minimal level, societal expectations define a mother's role as providing for basic needs and keeping a child safe, but children's needs far exceed these minimal expectations. Nurturing the growth and development of children requires putting the child's physical and emotional needs first. Yet parents must find ways of meeting children's needs while continuing to grow, develop, and meet their own needs. The capacity to balance the needs of children with ones own needs before one has "put away childish things" or become economically independent is at the heart of the concern about teen parents. A concern frequently expressed about teenage mothers is their expectations that a baby will meet their emotional needs, not that they will be faced with responding to the needs of a dependent and demanding baby.

Levels of Parental Conception

I, therefore, was surprised to find responsibility such a dominant theme in the interviews. Some respondents reported that they had become mothers to make them responsible, whereas others viewed the duties of motherhood as a continuation of the responsibility for child care and household duties they had assumed at a very early age. Still others reported that the reality about the long-term commitment of parenthood only dawned on them after the birth of the baby. Their perceptions of "being responsible" can be classified according to a cognitive-developmental classification of parents' concepts of children and the parental role developed by Newberger (1977). Based on interviews with a diverse group of parents, Newberger described four levels of parental understanding.

Egoistic parental conceptions are characterized by the ascendance of parental comforts and concerns above child's needs: "The organizing principle is achieving what the parent wants and the object of socialization of the child is maximum parental comfort" (Newberger, 1977: 3).

Conventional parental conceptions see the child's actions in relation to externally derived expectations. The parent's role is based on society's definition of what is correct and responsible. The parent differentiates the child's behavior in terms of bad, good, and normal. Child/parent roles are defined and parental comfort is secondary to parental responsibility.

Subjective-individualistic parental conceptions attribute to the child unique as well as universally shared qualities. The parent tries to understand the world from the child's perspective and in terms of the child's particular needs rather than in terms of role definitions.

Analytic parental conceptions, in Newberger's scheme, represent the most highly developed stage of parenting. The relationship between parent and child is viewed as mutual and reciprocal. The roles of parent and child are growing and developing ones wherein the parent's needs and the child's needs are balanced so that both sets of needs can be met.

Among teenage mothers one might expect to find a poorly developed sense of parenthood. Adolescent mothers are still in a stage of development characterized by self-absorption and identity issues. "Children having children" conveys the idea that one does not expect the conception of motherhood to be well developed in persons who are chronologically children themselves. Conventional wisdom portrays the teen mother as having a baby to have someone to love her or as thinking of a baby as a doll, not a dependent creature needing constant care. Although these less developed parental conceptions may have been held by some respondents before they had a child, at the time they were interviewed, few mothers exhibited the lowest level of parental conception.

At the time of the interview, Tracy, nineteen, and a school dropout, was one parent whose behavior partly fit Newberger's description of an egoistic parent. She was having a difficult time letting her children's needs take precedence over her own. Tracy is the mother of a boy two years old and a six-week-old baby. She had moved to her aunt's apartment a week before she was interviewed. The move was precipitated by an argument with her maternal grandmother with whom she has lived since infancy. When I called Tracy to follow up on a broken appointment, her grandmother told me that she had asked Tracy to leave her apartment that same day. Tracy did not take the children with her. Her grandmother reported that Tracy was very disrespectful when questioned about a boyfriend with whom she was spending time at the expense of her children's care. Tracy's two-year-old son was not talking and needs special help. Now sixty-three, Tracy's grandmother said she had been good to Tracy but did not want to take her disrespect any more, especially since she was taking a risk by letting Tracy and her children live with her in violation of the rules of the housing development.

Two weeks after this conversation, I interviewed Tracy in her aunt's crowded and poorly kept apartment where Tracy and the baby were staying temporarily. Although Tracy was having a difficult time being the kind of mother her grandmother thought she should be, she reported that she had been happy about her first pregnancy. Tracy said, "I just wanted to see how it was to be a mother. I was happy. My life was mostly empty. I felt like there was something missing. If I finished school and I got my two kids and everything. Now my life is a little bit more full."

Interviewer: You think kids make your life fuller?
Tracy: Yeah, I wanted to see how it was to have responsibility.
Interviewer: Had you had any responsibility before?
Tracy: Not really. None but taking care of my own self.

Although Tracy wanted to have children to make her life full and to have responsibility, she was overwhelmed with the care of an infant and a son with developmental problems. She explained that her son had been evaluated and his lack of speech development was not due to a hearing problem. She was not sure which hospital the speech therapist who had visited her son at her grandmother's house came from. She admitted she did not know how her grandmother understood what her son wanted most of the time because she usually did not understand him and depended on nonverbal cues.

Though Tracy's son was visiting in the apartment below, she did not ask if I wanted to see him. This was unusual, because most of the mothers wanted me to see their child(ren), and some showed me pictures if the child was not at home. Her infant son, a robust and attractive child, lay on the couch or was held by Tracy's sixteen-year-old sister, who told me she was pregnant and already had one child. Tracy, too, said she wanted to have more children. She did not express her thoughts about the fact that she had no permanent place to live, had not completed high school, had no job and no plans to marry.

Tracy's energies were focused on her relationship with the fathers of her two children. She reported that she still saw both of them but that she prefers the seventeen-year-old father of her second baby. He is an entertainer in a group that sings and dances, which she described as successful and "hoping to make it big." Tracy wants to have four more children before she is thirty so that she will not be "too old" with her last child: "I want them to try to grow up with me, like my mother and me. Even though I wasn't there with her, it was still like I grew up with her." She expressed no aspirations for the two children she already has. When asked what ambitions she had for them, she said she had never really thought about it. Tracy completed tenth grade but did not return to school after the birth of her first baby. She aspires to be an accountant but has no definite plans to return to school. Tracy talked about both fathers of her children wanting more children. Of the father of her second child, she said, "A daughter would make his life complete."

In the two years since she had her first child, Tracy had lived with the child's father at his mother's house, then with her grandmother, and now with her aunt. She describes the twenty-year-old father of her first child as good-looking, spoiled by women who take care of him, involved with drugs, and "wouldn't give me a dime."

She thinks the father of her second child is "too young" for her to expect anything of him. It was my impression that stability for Tracy's sons depended on her grandmother's willingness and capability to continue to provide care for them. In having responsibility for Tracy's children, Tracy's grandmother was facing a situation similar to that which led her to take custody of Tracy when she was an infant. Tracy reports that her grandmother took custody of her because "my mother was running the street. She'd take me with her and I got pneumonia and stuff like that when I was a little baby. I didn't know my mother was my mother 'til I was seven. I was sort of upset by it at first." Tracy is aware that her grandmother and grandfather are very disappointed in her. They had been strict with her. Her grandfather had supervised her homework. She reports that they had been more upset that she dropped out of school than that she got pregnant because she had done well in school and they had expected that she would go to college. Tracy appears to be attempting to make her life full by having children without the inner or outer resources to be a fully responsible mother. Her grandmother and grandfather had tried to protect her from early motherhood by being strict, but during adolescence, Tracy had looked to her mother rather than her grandmother as a role model. She reported that she seeks her mother's advice about men and other personal matters.

The complexity of Tracy's family life was dramatically illustrated when she talked about her father, who did not marry her mother and with whom she had had only sporadic contact. A fireman, he was stabbed to death when Tracy was eleven. She reports remembering the day and hour when she found out. Tracy then produced a yellowed newspaper clipping with a picture of her father and a report of the circumstances of his death. In spite of her nomadic existence and the apparent chaos of her belongings, she has kept this eight-year-old article about her father's murder.

Sandy, whose words open this chapter, like Tracy, is the mother of two children by different fathers and has not had stable living arrangements. Sandy, like Tracy, had wanted responsibility. Unlike Tracy, Sandy has been able to accomplish her goal. In her own judgment, she did not achieve her goal of becoming a responsible mother until after the birth of her second child. Sandy's description of herself as a mother to her first child shows that she is keenly aware that she had put her own convenience and needs before her child's.

   After the birth of her first child when she was sixteen Sandy had joined the Independent Living Program, a residential alternative for runaways, to escape a troubled home. She stayed there after the birth of her first child but was forced to leave when she violated the rules by becoming sexually involved with a young man in the house. The couple was asked to leave the program and went to live with his aunt. He later fathered her second child. He turned out to be abusive, and the aunt's apartment in public housing was dark and dirty. Sandy's daughter narrowly escaped death from a life-threatening illness caused by a combination of poor living conditions and neglect. When her daughter recovered, Sandy, pregnant with her second child, moved to a shelter and voluntarily placed her daughter in temporary foster care. Sandy, when asked what her children meant to her, replied,

> My kids? Responsibility. [Laughter.] I never had any responsibility before. Before I had Kay, I didn't have a care in the world. I came and I went when I pleased, and now it's not a shock any more because I've been doing it for a few years now. But when I first did it, I was living in the Independent Living Program, and I would kinda dump Kay on them, you know, they would babysit for you whenever you wanted to go somewhere. And I was constantly wanting to go somewhere, and they were babysitting for me like five days a week. I saw Kay every day, but I didn't sit down and play with her long enough to notice the development of the child, things that they did, or things that they liked or didn't like.

Sandy felt that she could correct the mistakes she had made with Kay. Before her son was born, she received a housing certificate for a subsidized apartment. For Sandy, housing was essential because her not having a place of her own had contributed to Kay's neglect and subsequent foster care. Without stable living arrangements Sandy could not be the responsible parent she wanted to be. Sandy's behavior as a mother to her first child had been focused on her own comfort rather than on her daughter's needs. Before Sandy had a second child, she went through a thoughtful decision-making process:

I wanted to have Karl because I had just got Section Eight [refers to a certificate that allows one to find a subsidized apartment in the private market], and I remember I had planned to have an abortion. I had an appointment all set up for an abortion for him when I first found out [about the housing certificate], because I didn't want to be in a shelter when I had him. So I was going to have an abortion, and like the day before I was supposed to get my abortion, I got a phone call saying my Section Eight had come through, and come fill out all the papers and stuff next week. I said, "Oh, my God! God must really want me to have this baby." [Laughter.] So I said, "I'm going to have this baby!" And I went down there and did everything I had to do. And by the time I was four months pregnant, I looked for an apartment twenty-four hours a day. I didn't sleep for a week, and I came out here and I found this apartment. I moved in here in February of '86. I was four months pregnant, then he came in July. I wanted to have him because I wanted to give him the kind of home I never gave Kay. She's moved around so much for a baby, and she's been in at least eight or nine places and some of them without me. And that's awful. And like now, I'm so glad she's stable. She comes in—it makes me feel so good when she runs to the steps and she knows where she lives and she sleeps in the same bed every night. Everything is just so much more situated now.

Sandy admits that her pregnancies were accidental, but she thinks they did lead her to develop a sense of responsibility. She candidly evaluates her behavior when Kay was a baby as irresponsible. Sandy reflected on how having children was a positive, maturing experience:

I needed to turn around and that [having children] did it. You know, the minute I had Kay that didn't take place, but in the long run, I wanted it to make me develop responsibility, and that's what it did. By the time that Kay was one, I was pretty much on my way there. And now that she's going on three, I'm even more, well by the time she was two actually, 'cause when she was one, I was still going through my foster care stuff. But by the time she was two, I was fine. Now a year later, I'm ten times better than I was then.

It took courage and maturity to voluntarily give up her daughter for two months because she was homeless. During Kay's stay in foster care, Sandy had visited her daily and had taken her to her mother's on weekends. By the time I met Sandy, she actually enjoyed her children and was able to appreciate their growth and stability. Sandy's life also illustrates that children's needs may have a better chance of being met if a mother's basic needs such as education, housing, and job training are met.

Other teen mothers defined being a good mother by contrasting their own behavior with teen mothers who were not responsible. A responsible mother is a good mother because she does not "run the streets," take drugs, physically neglect her children, or expect her mother or others to take care of her children. A responsible mother realizes that she is no longer able to freely participate in the usual teenage activities. Being a good mother was identified by Schwab (1983) as a route to responsible adulthood among white rural adolescents in New England. Motherhood, according to Schawb, was a means of conferring responsibility that transformed the adolescents into adults. Beth and Joyce see their status as mothers as conferring responsibility, which to them means that adolescent activities are secondary to parental responsibility.

Beth, fifteen when her first child was born, is the mother of a two-year-old and an infant. When asked what it is like to be a mother, she replied, "Certain things you used to do before you had kids you can't do now, unless you was the type that didn't care, as somebody who was partying all the time."

Beth perceived her choices before having babies in terms of physical freedom, coming and going as she pleased. If her kids were not invited to places, she stayed at home reporting that "where they're not welcome, I'm not welcome."

Joyce, twenty, and the mother of two children, had ambivalent feelings about having a second baby:

> I felt depressed sometimes, and sometimes I felt happy because God gifted me with two kids. And I felt kind of sad 'cause I thought I'm having two kids now. I can't do everything I want to do. Some of the things I could do, but, you know you can't do everything that you always did when you was free. Like roller skating. I love to go roller skating. Roller skating and like, you know, go out with friends, go to movies and everything. You have to slow down because you got *big* responsibilities.

Joyce recognizes that she has responsibilities now that she is the mother of two children, but she wishes she could do the things she likes to do. The struggle Joyce has between the desire to be an unburdened teenager and the need to fulfill the role expected of a "conventional" parent was evident in her behavior during our interview.

Joyce's two-year-old daughter cried throughout the interview. The interview was early in the morning, and the child had not been given breakfast. She repeatedly asked her mother for juice or cereal, tugging at her to go to the kitchen. Joyce did not respond to her daughter until I asked if she would like to stop the interview and prepare food for her. This pattern of unresponsiveness continued throughout the interview. Nevertheless, Joyce said that being a mother "means you can't think about yourself any more. You've got to think about two kids now because you got two responsibilities." Joyce perceives herself as a responsible and responsive mother. She works between forty and fifty hours per week at the checkout counter of a department store, depending on her aunt, a neighbor, and her mother for childcare. Her mother thinks that Joyce should not be working because caring for Joyce's two children, her own young sons, and two foster children is too much work. When I asked Joyce whether she enjoys her children, she replied that she takes them shopping and to the park on her day off. Joyce is trying to mix the roles of mother and worker successfully. Work allows her to support her children but requires her to depend on others to care for her children. She is attempting to meet her needs and her children's needs at the same time. Joyce's dilemma is a common one for mothers of young children. Teen mothers, like other mothers, exhibit a number of ways of coping with the responsibility of motherhood. Some, like Joyce, work and depend on relatives for child care, whereas others, like Agnes, eighteen, are happy to be with their children but also have plans for learning a trade. Agnes not only meets her children's needs, but has an individualistic parental conception that allows her to differentiate between her children and to see things from the child's perspective.

During the interview, Agnes' children were present. The baby, seven months old, needed to be fed, and her sixteen-month-old girl, napping in another part of the house, needed to be checked on. Agnes asked if we could interrupt the interview so that she could warm a bottle and feed the baby while we talked. When she thought she heard noises from her daughter's bedroom, she excused herself and checked on her. She talked about the children in a way that showed an understanding of their development and a pride in their accomplishments. She thinks that motherhood is "fun sometimes but also difficult and frustrating." Agnes thinks that as a mother she has to "share feelings and thoughts and communicate with the children." Agnes is pleased she completed high school and wants to get more education because she wants to be able to teach her children. Agnes's responsive manner was reflected in the alert, calm, and happy demeanor of the children. Agnes is glad she had her children now instead of later. She does not see them as holding her back " 'cause when they're both old enough, I can still go on with my education. And I don't feel they'll stop me, because I did finish high school."

Like Agnes, Emma, whose two-year-old son was born when she was seventeen, sees the unique needs of her child and tries to understand the world from his perspective. Her concept of parenthood also encompasses the most highly developed level of parenting: seeing the child as a complex system with his/her own psychological needs. She explained that one of the reasons she and her son's father do not get along is because his mother "wants to be his life. She doesn't want anybody else for him but her." Emma will not let the grandmother have a part in raising her child because she does not approve of her parenting. Emma's conception of a child's needs are expressed in her evaluation of her son's paternal grandmother's treatment of her own ten-year-old son:

> She works. And there's nothing wrong with working, but the type of work she does, she's a sitter. She goes to someone else's house and takes care of their kid and their house and then when she comes home, she doesn't want to be bothered. Well, I can understand that she's worked hard all day and she doesn't want to be bothered. But her responsibility is to her younger son first. She was there for my son's father. But she sort of does the same thing with his little brother that she does with him. They spend too much time with just him and her. *He never leaves the house—the little brother. You know, like when kids are young, they need to experi-*

ence other children, experience right and wrong. She doesn't allow him to get space. He is in the house beside her twenty-four hours a day. He's ten years old now. On holidays, they spend the holidays, him and her. No other family whatsoever, and she has a very big family so I feel there's no reason. My family is very important to me and I share all my holidays and any special occasion. *I don't feel that any kid should have to spend so much time with that parent. That could be like a punishment. Because I know there were times when my mother and I didn't get along, and I just couldn't wait to get away from her. His mother is very possessive. He's not allowed to go anywhere. He can go and play if she sits in front of the house. But he can't go where she can't see him. So, therefore, he can't play with other kids because their parents allow them to go in the field and play.*

Here Emma reveals that a responsible mother gives a child autonomy and freedom so that he can learn from his peers and develop a sense of ethics. She realizes that children do not learn in isolation and that it is best for a mother not to be possessive. Emma thinks that work should not interfere with meeting the emotional needs of a child, and Emma's life illustrates that mothers may have a career.

Emma's mother has always worked, and Emma is planning a career for herself. She attends a health careers training program while her son is in day care. At nineteen, Emma has developed an analytic parental conception. She is responsibly meeting her son's needs while continuing with her own education and self-development.

Arlene and her fiancé, with whom she lives, have a well-planned system of childcare and child rearing. They see Arlene's son as a unique person with his own psychological and physical needs. They cooperate to best meet the child's needs and still carry on their responsibilities. Arlene is a college student, and her fiancé owns a business. She describes her three-year-old son as attached to her and having to adjust to being in day care:

At day care he had a lot of trouble because when I dropped him off, he wouldn't let me leave. He didn't want me to go until I reassured him, "Yes, dear, I'm coming back tonight to get you." And you see, they wouldn't let you leave unless he would sit in his

chair. And now, my son has this psychological thing in his mind—
"I know my mother cannot leave unless I'm sitting down"—so he
won't sit down. Just last month my fiancé and I agreed that he's
going to drop him off, not me. So now my fiancé drops him off. It's
a lot better. He has no problems. He goes right in, washes his
hands, and sits down.

Arlene proudly described her son as "very bright." She likes to
teach him how to spell and she thinks that he has one of the best
developed vocabularies of the children in day care. When asked
what she wanted for her son, she replied, "Education is at the top of
the list. And self-worth, a positive attitude, and a lot of self-esteem."

Self-Esteem

Arlene probably has a good chance of accomplishing these goals for
her son. She is a successful college student and an artist. She has the
support of her extended family and the man with whom she lives.
Arlene has a lot to be proud of, but the event she reported as making
her feel great was being chosen to represent her neighborhood
health center parenting program at a national conference, where she
talked about her experience as a teen mother. Her extemporaneous
speech was a milestone for her: it was the first time she admitted to
herself that the father of her son was not going to come back and
marry her. Up until the conference, she told others and herself that
she actually had a date for his return, that they had an apartment
and were getting married. Telling others about her experience
allowed Arlene to face the truth and "get on with her life." Arlene
is full of hope and self-confidence as a result of a series of self-
affirming experiences. She is successful in college, had one of her
graphic designs on display in a local museum, and is engaged to be
married to a twenty-eight-year-old man who is successful in his
work. Arlene volunteers for the teen parent program at the high
school from which she graduated. She designs the brochure for the
program and talks to teenage mothers about her experiences.
   According to conventional wisdom, teenagers who have babies
often do not have a good opinion of themselves. This study gathered

only retrospective data on events that may contribute to a positive self-evaluation. Content analysis of responses to the question, "Do you remember a time or an event when you felt great about yourself?" are reported in tabular form in Table 6–1. Excerpts from responses to this question and respondents' self-selected reports of events and relationships give a fuller understanding of how respondents feel about themselves. As Table 6–1 indicates, 47 percent of the respondents reported having and taking care of a baby as the event that made them feel best about themselves. Twenty percent reported an educational event, and 7 percent said that working made them feel best about themselves, whereas 23 percent reported other types of events, such as speaking in public or singing in the church choir. Only one respondent could think of nothing that made her feel good about herself.

Respondents associate credibility, competence, and independence with the events that enhance self-esteem. For example, to Cher, having a baby enhanced self-esteem because the new status of motherhood conferred credibility on her. All the people important to her treated her with new respect: "When I became pregnant, they listened more to what I had to say. 'She's pregnant now, listen to her, this and that.' I don't think it really hit me at first, but at the hospital when I had him, I told myself, WOW, I'm a mother! I was happy; I was excited; I was really totally excited. I was shocked; I was surprised; like wow, I really have a baby. *I just gave birth to a baby!*"

Table 6–1
Positive Self-Esteem Events by Number of Children

| Type of Event | Number of Children | | Total | |
	One	Two	Number	Percentage
Having a Baby	8	6	14	47
Educational	2	4	6	20
Work	1	1	2	7
Other	4	3	7	23
None	0	1	1	3
Total	15	15	30	100

Cher reported that her sisters, boyfriend, mother, father, cousins, and other relatives listened to her during her pregnancy and after she gave birth. Her mother "spoiled" her by buying her all sorts of things and doing things for her.

Just as pregnancy and birth gave Cher credibility in terms of significant others, the physical act of having two babies and following up on their care made Liz feel competent: "I felt great when I had my two kids that they was all right and everything. I felt real good. And the time I felt the best was when they was born and they was out of me. Boy, that was the best relief in your life! And when my kids have appointments and *I would make myself known,* and go to the appointments and get there, I felt extra good. I felt great."

For Annie, similar feelings of competence came from giving birth, because she endured labor and delivered a healthy baby: "When I delivered I felt real great because most of my friends had c-sections and they couldn't even deliver. And I actually delivered a nine pounder. And on top of that the lady told me out of all the babies she delivered, I did great because of my age. I did what I was supposed to do. I had over twenty-five hours of labor, which was painful. She said I did good."

Despite this positive experience, Annie doubted that she could achieve her aspirations to be an obstetrician. She feels that she is not smart enough to go to college, so she thinks she might like to be a midwife but is uncertain about the training required. In spite of these aspirations, Annie, who was in her senior year when she was interviewed, said she would most likely get training to operate computers. Annie perceived herself as smart enough to have a baby but not smart enough to be a doctor or even a midwife.

Annie's low opinion of herself was exacerbated by the way her son's father had treated her. They were fourteen and in the seventh grade when she became pregnant. Annie says she and her son's father are enemies. He had done so many terrible things to her that she said she could not talk about them. He was her boyfriend for almost five years and during that time he got two other girls pregnant. Annie now does not trust men and feels that is why she broke up with her most recent boyfriend. She and her most recent boyfriend are still friends, and he makes her feel great: "Before I met him, I just felt I wasn't good enough for anyone. My son's father said a lot of negative stuff to me and it stayed in my head. So I didn't think I was *good* enough to go with anybody else. When I met him, I felt positive, he made me feel positive about myself." Annie is striving to feel good about herself, but her primary goal is to make her mother have a good opinion of her: "I want to get further than my mother in life so she'll be proud of me. So she'll say, 'She did it.' I like her to compliment me."

Several respondents reported an educational achievement as the event that made them feel best about themselves. Some respondents who were still in high school remember graduating from the eighth grade as the time they felt best about themselves. For example, Margie recalled, "When I graduated from the eighth grade, I felt happy that I made it. I'll feel more happy when I finish high school. The second time was when I had the baby. I felt proud he came out okay." Margie had an eight pound twelve ounce baby when she was fifteen. A senior in an adult evening diploma program when she was interviewed, Margie planned to enroll in a training program and work during the summer. She had begun to explore programs at local colleges. She has two brothers who attend a state college. It is the family's expectation (including her father, who did not marry her mother and separated from her when Margie was five), that she too must go to college. Her father invited her to live with him out West and attend college there.

Some respondents remembered relatives who helped them when their self-esteem was low. Ivy reports her aunt had treated her like "somebody" when she was eleven or twelve and "when I felt like I was no one, when I felt like killing myself. Nobody was there. My mom works, was going to school, she's out. My brother and sister weren't around; they had their love life." Ivy had entered her teen years feeling bad about herself. In a previous section, I reported on Ivy's subsequent depression and lack of supervision during her teen years. A poor self-image contributed to Ivy's early sexual involvement. Her self-esteem may have been higher had she not felt abandoned. A multiplicity of factors contributed to Ivy's feelings about herself, and some of these same factors, such as loneliness and lack of supervision, played a part in her becoming a teenage mother. Ivy is completing high school in an adult learning program and working part-time.

The event Ivy described as making her feel good about herself is often considered a typical rite of passage by American adolescents: "When I first decided I wanted to get my driver's license and I went to driver's ed and paid for it all by myself, my mom didn't help me any, and I finished it and got my license and I learned to drive. When I first got that, I felt great about that. Then I bought my car. I paid for it all by myself. It's all paid for. It's in my name. It was good. I felt independent then. I didn't need my mother or father to give me any money for it" (Quinn, Newfield, and Protinsky, 1985). Here Ivy combined a typical teenage accomplishment of getting a driver's license with the adult responsibility of working and paying for her car.

These excerpts illustrate that there is no one route to self-esteem but that self-affirming experiences are necessary for growth, development, and achievement. These respondents and their parents have hopes that they will complete school and "make something of themselves." I heard over and over in the interviews statements such as, "I just want to make a mark in life"; "I want my mother to be proud of me"; or "I want to be able to show my kids that I did something."

When avenues for achieving credibility, competence, and independence are not sufficiently available to adolescents, pregnancy and motherhood might be a means of attaining these goals, but whereas nearly half the respondents looked to childbearing for a positive experience, half also identified education, work, and other events as self-affirming. Many respondents, like Margie, found motherhood self-affirming but not to the exclusion of school and work.

In addition to the narrative responses, respondents were administered a self-esteem questionnaire from which a self-esteem score was derived. Miller (1983) used this self-esteem questionnaire in a Child Welfare League study, a study conducted between 1979 and 1982 in Chicago, Cleveland, and Minneapolis with an 85 percent black sample of 127 teen mothers who were under age sixteen at the time of their first birth. The questions are a combination of items based on Rosenberg's (1965) Self-Esteem Scale and Coopersmith's (1967) Self-Esteem Inventory, both considered reliable indicators of self-esteem. In the CWLA study, the self-esteem questionnaire was administered twice, resulting in mean scores of 53 and 52.2. These

Table 6–2
Self-Esteem

	Score	Age at First Birth	Number of Children	Education	Father Support	Family Support
Shelly	41	15	1	0	0	1
Virginia	42	15	2	0	0	1
Robin	45	15	1	0	0	1
Joyce	46	18	2	0	1	1
Kate	46	15	2	1	1	1
Penny	47	17	2	0	1	1
Natalie	48	17	2	0	0	1
Annie	48	15	1	1	0	1
Krista	49	17	2	1	1	1
Grace	50	15	2	0	1	1
Tracy	50	17	2	0	0	1
Cher	50	17	1	1	1	1
Emma	50	17	1	1	1	1
Liz	52	16	2	1	0	1
Robbie	52	16	1	1	0	1
Dee	53	16	2	0	1	1
Margie	53	15	1	1	0	1
Beth	54	15	2	0	0	1
Corrie	54	16	2	1	0	1
Nellie	54	16	1	1	1	1
Linda	54	17	1	1	0	0
Ivy	55	17	1	1	0	1
Jackie	55	17	1	1	1	1
Hattie	55	17	1	1	1	1
Loretta	56	15	1	1	0	1
Mae	57	16	2	0	1	1
Sandy	58	16	2	1	0	0
Peggy	59	18	1	1	1	1
Agnes	63	17	2	1	1	1
Arlene	68	17	1	1	0	1

Possible Range = 18–72
Actual Range = 41–68
Mean = 52.1
Median = 52

Education   0 = Dropout
                1 = Graduated or In School
Father Support   0 = No
                1 = Yes
Family Support   0 = No
                1 = Yes

are considered positive self-esteem scores. Miller correlated the
scores with a number of variables and found that the scores varied
by race, with black teens achieving higher scores than did white
respondents.

As Table 6–2 indicates, the mean self-esteem score for my sample is 52, the same as the mean score for the CWLA study respondents. The possible range of scores is 18–72. The CWLA scores
ranged from 33 to 68 in the first interview, and from 32 to 65 in the
second interview, while the range among my respondents was
41–68.

The relation between self-esteem and three separate factors—
number of children, support from fathers, and high school completion—is reported in Table 6–3. Although the difference between the
self-esteem scores of mothers with one baby and those with two
babies proved not to be statistically significant, respondents with
one baby had a slightly higher mean score of 53 compared to 51 for
mothers of two babies. Also there was no statistically significant
difference between the self-esteem scores of mothers who received
support from the fathers of their child(ren) compared to mothers
who received no support. The mean score for fourteen respondents

Table 6–3
Average Self-Esteem by Selected Characteristics

Selected Characteristics	Number of Respondents	Mean	Standard Deviation	df	t-Value	Probabilit
Number of Children						
One baby	15	53	6.188	28	.815	.4217
Two babies	15	51.3	5.431			
Father's Support						
No father support	16	51.8	6.713	28	−.373	.7121
Father support	14	52.4	4.897			
Level of High School Completed						
No high school	11	48.5	4.967	28	−2.99	.0058*
High school	19	54.3	5.216			

*p ≤ .01

difference between the self-esteem scores of mothers who
support from the fathers of their child(ren) compared to moth
who received no support. The mean score for fourteen respondents
who received support is 52.4 compared to 51.8 for those not receiving support. (Support includes informal and formal material support and emotional involvement with the mother and/or child[ren].)

The relationship between self-esteem and education proved to
be statistically significant at the .0058 level. The average self-esteem
score for the nineteen women who have completed or who are
enrolled in high school is 54.3 compared to 48.5 for the eleven
women who have not completed high school and were not enrolled
in school when they were interviewed.

The responsibility of parenthood emerged as a persistent theme.
Contrary to conventional wisdom, these young mothers did not
treat their babies as dolls or have unrealistic expectations about the
love a baby was capable of giving them. Most of the mothers were
responsible parents who put the needs of their children before their
own convenience. Several of the thirty young mothers experienced
motherhood as a maturing experience. They were proud mothers
who frequently associated childbearing and educational achievement with happiness and self-esteem.

7
Beyond the Family

I don't really think there's activities after school or anything like that out there. They have suicide hot lines, AIDS hot lines, sexual hot lines, but all these hot lines are on telephones. You don't want a telephone. People are not there—it's not a good option. I think there should be a program that would teach you about life and show you. If it was right after school, kids would deal with it. People don't really want to leave and come back again. If you've got them there, everybody would want to go because everybody wants to talk.

—Ivy, a mother at seventeen.

Family, school, church, and community have traditionally been considered the most significant environments for the shaping of any individual's life. Having looked at the family life of respondents, especially the parenting behavior of the respondents' mothers and fathers, we turn now to community institutions and the neighborhood, the outer context of respondents' lives. Schools, health care institutions, and public welfare are the systems most frequently used by these young mothers. Just as love, acceptance, and discipline make families the first locus of nurturing ties, institutional representatives such as teachers, social workers, and health care providers help a child move beyond the family into a larger world.

Institutional arrangements shape the troubles people experience in private life (Mills, 1959). Personal situations are best understood in the context of environmental factors. These perspectives on personal dilemmas are also reflected in the recognition that physical, psychological, and social well-being are influenced by income, housing conditions, neighborhood safety, and the presence and quality of neighborhood institutions.

School

After the family, the institution where children spend the greatest amount of time is the school. Public education stands at the center of American culture as a universal service for all citizens. Public schools have been the doorway to upward social mobility and opportunity for generations of immigrants and descendants of slaves. The importance of education to the black community is evident in the significance attached to the 1954 *Brown* v. *Board of Education* Supreme Court decision, which declared segregated schools unconstitutional. The decades since the decision have been marked by a sometimes violent social struggle regarding its implementation, particularly the busing of children to schools outside their neighborhoods. Whites blamed busing for the destruction of the character of the neighborhood school, but little attention was paid to the effects of busing on the black neighborhood. As a result of busing, blacks too lost the supportive character of the neighborhood school. Busing imposed an additional burden on already fragile families. Offering schoolchildren a better education by busing them to suburban communities resulted in some parents having no access to the institutions where their children were being educated. Ironically, one of the reasons black parents had supported busing was because Boston schools were inaccessible to parents. Actual physical access was made nearly impossible because schools were locked once the children were inside. There was no active parent/teacher association. Also, most teachers were white and not from the neighborhood; most black parents felt these teachers exhibited little understanding of the families or the neighborhood. Schools with children locked inside and parents locked out became a symbol of the relationship between the schools and black parents during the sixties.

During the mid-seventies, after court-ordered busing, Boston became a national symbol of resistance to school integration. This era fell at the beginning of the educational careers of most of my respondents. One alternative for some black parents was to send their children to suburban schools. Nellie, Dee, and Emma had attended suburban schools, which created problems for all of them. Nellie found her school nice "but you have a lot of prejudiced people." Expecting to hear about racial prejudice, I asked Nellie how the prejudice had been exhibited. She replied, "Like one girl this year got pregnant, and she had to leave the school because she was pregnant. As soon as they found out, they sent her away." This incident occurred after Nellie had left the school. When she discovered she was pregnant, Nellie did not attempt to finish the school year there, but transferred to a school for pregnant girls. She liked "pregnant school" because it "wasn't prejudiced," and she learned about childbirth and what to do after the baby was born in addition to academic subjects.

Dee also transferred to a school for pregnant girls. She preferred the special school because "I was out there with all those white kids and stuff. I guess when you get around people you know, you feel better. I didn't know nobody out there." Although Dee and Nellie had not felt as alienated from the neighborhood as had Emma, they, too, had not had neighborhood friends because they attended suburban schools.

Emma had attended a suburban school from first through ninth grade. She transferred from her suburban school to a neighborhood school because her mother was unable to be involved in school activities. Emma dropped out during her pregnancy:

I was in the eleventh grade and I was probably six months pregnant. We had moved, so there was no way for me to get to school actually. And I didn't want to go to school where we were, so I kind of just let it go at that. I had gone to METCO [a program that buses black inner-city students to suburban schools] from first grade until my freshman year in high school, and then I transferred to English. And it was a big difference. I transferred because it was a hassle for my mother. I mean, because you had to go to meetings, and if you didn't go to so many meetings, then it was a big hassle. She couldn't really be involved in things I did at school because she didn't have a car and she couldn't get out there. There were no buses running or anything. It was rough on her. So when my sister graduated that next year, she took us out. All of us were in METCO except for my older brother. *We definitely got a better education. But it also made it harder for me to adjust in the outside world. From first grade to my freshman year, by the time I got home from school, it was dark outside. It was time to come in and*

*do my homework and go to bed. So I never really got to know
what it was like. To me life was living in the suburbs and it was
totally different. I lived here* [a large public housing project], *but
I didn't know anybody.* We very rarely spent the summers here. So
it was difficult. Sometimes I'd spend a couple of weeks with my
father or my stepfather; or I'd go to California and spend it with
my aunt. So it was a big adjustment when I went into English
High. *I could not adjust.* I mean every time I turned around it
seemed like someone was starting trouble, someone wanted to
fight. And I never liked school anyway. I was your average student. I could have done better, but I never liked school so I didn't
socialize in school. I went to class. I didn't have any friends in
school. Probably if I had done those things, I would have done a
lot better in school. But I didn't like school. So I felt I was here to
do one thing. I'll just do it and get out of here as fast as I could. So
when I went to English, that was it. School was something that I
just learned to adjust to. Even when I was little, I was close to my
mother and I always wanted to be home with her. *I never wanted
to go to school.*

Emma's story is extraordinary. It is hard to imagine a first
grader who is nearly phobic about school coping with attending a
school inaccessible to her mother for virtually all of her school
career. Staying in school under these circumstances represents a
strong commitment to education. Emma's description of being
bused to a suburb and having no identification with her neighborhood is an indication of the social price some black city children pay
to get a quality education unattainable at their neighborhood
school. Although Emma had never liked school, a suburban school
had offered her a chance to learn in an orderly atmosphere.

Emma's pregnancy occurred after she transferred to her neighborhood high school. At this time in her life, school and home were
chaotic. At school someone was always wanting to fight and "things
were bad at home. I guess you could say I sort of felt like there was
no love in my house." As conditions worsened at home, it is possible
that the continuity and order that her suburban school provided
would have prevented pregnancy and dropping out. Emma admits
she had a baby for the wrong reasons, but she does not feel that it
ruined her life.

Emma completed high school through a GED program and continues to pursue her goal of obtaining a college degree by attending a program to prepare for college. She described the program as an interim step to get her accustomed to a schedule again after having been at home for so long with her son. Emma is confident that she will get a college degree and become a registered nurse. Having one child and day-care services makes it likely that Emma will be able to achieve her educational aspirations.

Unlike Nellie, Dee, and Emma, other respondents attended school in Boston. Some experienced chaos and disorder, whereas others did not. Mae, an eighteen-year-old mother of two, completed ninth grade in a Boston neighborhood known to be hostile to integration:

> They let you take your own responsibility into your hands. They actually let you run wild. I wasn't used to it. I was used to discipline, like in elementary and middle school where you had to stand in line and wait your turn. *South Boston High was a zoo. The kids coming there, they made noise and some of us couldn't learn because they wanted to act like jerks.* They used to call me "Miss Righteous." One thing, I was going to church. And another thing, when they made noise in the back, I was the one who would speak up. I was trying to learn. They wouldn't listen to the teachers. There were so many kids who were ready to fight the teacher. So I didn't like it for that reason. *Then when I got pregnant that was just a good old excuse to get out of there.*

Mae's negative experience in school has probably dampened her motivation to complete school. Mae did not return to school after the first baby was born, and now she has two children. Mae expressed her intention to enroll in a GED program. To carry out her intentions, Mae has to arrange for day care and transportation; more importantly, she has to overcome her negative feelings about school.

These excerpts indicate the difficulties facing black parents and teenagers in their educational decision making. Attendance in a suburban school assures a better quality of education, yet those who choose this option are faced with schools inaccessible to parents and alienation from the children in their neighborhoods. Students who stay in the city, like Mae, risk another kind of alienation—alienation from education itself. Some respondents, however, attach a new importance to education after having a baby. Kate was a runaway with a poor attendance record before she had her first child. Now she sees things differently:

> School is important because I don't want the kids to grow up and say that I never tried to finish school. *And it's hard to raise a kid on an eighth grade education.* Then you'd be trying to find a job with no high school diploma. They want high school diplomas. I just don't want my kids to come home and say, "Mommy, what's eight times eight?" and it's sixty-four, but you say, "I don't know." I have some friends that are in their twenties and their kids ask them and they can't answer. If you have a child and they come home and say, "Mommy, could you help me with this?" *it is real sad if you can't help your child. I just want to be educated for them.*

Kate, the mother of two children, was interviewed just before her seventeenth birthday. Having left school before completing eighth grade, she had tried to go back to regular school but "just couldn't." She enrolled in a GED program after the birth of the first baby. To attend the program, Kate spent weekdays with her grandmother, who kept the baby while she was in school. She returned to her mother's on weekends. She had not quite worked out the logistics of getting to the program with two children when I spoke with her, but she thought she might stay with her grandmother as she had done after her first baby was born, because her grandmother was closer to the bus line and would babysit. Kate was prepared to take both children on the bus if her program provided childcare.

The above excerpt indicates that Kate is motivated to finish high school, to get a job, and to help her children. Several respondents, like Kate, wanted to be able to help their children with school work. These young mothers worried that their children might see them as having done "nothing," thus their motivation to finish high school increased after childbirth, but finding the right program, childcare, and transportation made it difficult to act on the motivation. Kate is fortunate to have her grandmother as a resource. Even so, she has begun to lower her aspirations. Kate ideally would like to finish college, "but instead, I'm gonna stay at Bridge [the GED program] and do word processing."

Corrie and Agnes were good students. Thus, even two pregnancies did not deter them from completing high school. In junior high school, Corrie was placed in a program for the academically talented and was determined not to let her pregnancies interfere with graduation: "I had him in May, May 27th. I stayed home that week and then I went back. I took my finals. It was like, 'What are you doing?' I was like 'I gotta take my finals. I want to get promoted to the twelfth grade.' " Corrie was promoted and completed high school before her second baby was born. Unlike many respondents, she did not want to leave regular school for a maternity school: "They kept trying to put me into another school, but I said I'm gonna stay right here."

Like Corrie, Agnes's two births did not interfere with her schooling: "I went straight with both of them. I went to school every day. I got a tutor, too." Agnes's second baby was born in the spring. With the help of a tutor, she was able to accomplish her two main goals—graduating and going to the prom. Agnes mentioned that she wanted to complete school so that she could teach her children and show them "at least I finished high school."

Krista, one of five respondents with two children who completed high school, became pregnant during the last half of the eleventh grade and stayed in school. At the beginning of twelfth grade she went to maternity school and stayed out of school for a semester. Her sister babysat while Krista attended school. Corrie, Agnes, and Krista were at grade level and in their next to last year in school when they became pregnant. They had the support of their families for childcare. The expectations of respondents and the families that they would graduate were an important factor in teenage mothers staying in school. The other respondents with two children who completed high school are Sandy and Liz. Sandy was in an independent living program that also offered GED courses, whereas Liz went to a special maternity school during the latter months of both pregnancies and returned to public school.

Nine of the fifteen mothers with two children did not complete high school, moreover, they were in ninth or tenth grade when they became pregnant with their first child. Several of them, like Mae, had not had positive school experiences and would have been at least two years older than their classmates had they returned to school. In contrast, only two mothers with one child, Shelly and Robin, were school dropouts, but both were working full-time. All other respondents with one child were either in school or had completed high school, including two who attended college. Thus, age at birth of first child and number of children were related to school completion.

My findings are consistent with the Children's Defense Fund's suggestion that motivation and capacity to prevent teenage pregnancy are related to being at grade level and exhibiting good school performance (Children's Defense Fund, 1987). Findings from longitudinal data on Furstenberg's Baltimore study of three hundred teenage mothers indicate that being behind a grade level or two in school is a predictor of being at risk for early pregnancy. In the Baltimore study mothers who attended a special alternative school had better educational outcomes and more success in later life than those who did not (Furstenberg, Brooks-Gunn, and Morgan, 1987). The majority of respondents recognized the importance of completing high school as a minimum requirement for employment. More importantly, most felt that education has intrinsic value and makes one a better parent.

Health Care Institutions

Unlike children's relationship to school, which by law begins at age six and must continue until at least sixteen, their relationship to the health care system is periodic rather than continuous. Respondents' contact with the health care system is not documented prior to their pregnancies, but some respondents reported having access to contraceptive information and birth control pills prior to their pregnancies, whereas others had access to information and contraceptives only after giving birth. That most teenagers do not use contraceptives until after they have been sexually active for some time has led to increased attention to locating health clinics in schools in an effort to improve the general health of students, to lower fertility rates, to reduce pregnancies, and to encourage the postponement of sexual activity. Whereas all or some of these goals are widely accepted, school-based clinics are controversial because opponents view them narrowly as potential dispensers of contraceptives and see them as usurping parents' rights. Still others view clinics in schools as service duplication because of the established network of hospitals and neighborhood health centers.

All respondents in this study were related to a hospital and/or a neighborhood health center. The majority of respondents were located through Brigham and Women's Hospital and St. Margaret's Hospital. These mothers differ from teens who do not seek prenatal services early and go on to deliver in hospitals that do not follow up on their adolescent mothers. Brigham and Women's and St. Margaret's make special efforts to follow up teen mothers and connect them to other programs such as the Young Parents Program (YPP) at Children's Hospital. The Massachusetts Department of Public Health's Adolescent Pregnancy and Parenting Study, which collects data for two years after a teenager gives birth, may be an added incentive for hospitals and clinics to stay involved with teenage mothers. It is also common for Boston neighborhood health centers to have services and programs especially for teen mothers and their children. Several respondents had been taking their children to neighborhood health centers; whereas others had participated in the Young Parents Program at Children's Hospital designed to provide medical care for mothers and children. Respondents who had participated in this program liked the convenience of being able to have their own and the child's checkups in one appointment. The YPP also provided mothers with a telephone number so that they could have a quick response to any questions or problems. Hattie regrets that she is too old for the program and has to switch to another health care agency: "I liked it a lot. They were really nice. They talked to you, made sure you kept up with your birth control pills or whatever kind of contraceptive you were using. They took real good care of my son. Any kind of problems, you call this number and a beeper would go through and they would call you back and see what the problem was, and if it was really necessary for you to take him to the hospital."

Several respondents had participated in the YPP program described by Hattie. Except for one mother, respondents did not report participating in group meetings for parents and children that were offered by the social workers in the Brigham Adolescent Clinic.

Health care professionals at Brigham and Women's and St. Margaret's hospitals have made considerable efforts to involve pregnant teens in early prenatal care and follow-up after the baby is born. High mortality and low birth weight among black teen mothers cause special concern among health care professionals. Of the forty-five children born to the mothers in my sample, only two were premature. One baby's weight was under three pounds and the other baby weighed just under five pounds. But, 27 (60 percent) of the forty-five babies weighed seven pounds or more, which indicates the adequate health and nutrition of the thirty young mothers and the good medical care they received throughout their pregnancies.

Two mothers, Robin and Hattie, who delayed prenatal care until after six months, did not have low birth weight babies. Hattie's baby weighed almost nine pounds and is a bright, healthy three-year-old, whereas Robin's child, also three, is developmentally delayed. Robin did not acknowledge that her child was not developing normally. I observed that the child had no speech and was not curious about the tape recorder or crayons and paper I offered her. Robin had concealed her pregnancy to avoid pressure from her mother to get an abortion. She also reported that she had not eaten during her early pregnancy because she didn't want to gain weight and risk having her pregnancy discovered. Hattie, on the other hand, had made sure that she ate well. Hattie reported some confusion as to whether or not she was pregnant in the early months because she had been taking the pill and had a history of irregular periods, but she also did not want people to know. Hattie was very lucky to have reported for medical care when she did. She developed diabetes during the last months of her pregnancy and required special care to assure that she and the baby were healthy.

Respondents' contact with health care institutions paid off in healthy babies and mothers, but the birth control counseling proved not nearly so successful. At the time of the interview several respondents reported that they were not using birth control. Their reasons were that they were not involved with anyone now, that they were having side effects from the pill, or that they needed to get a new prescription.

Welfare and Work

Although the majority of respondents (23) receive AFDC, it was reported as the sole source of income for only three respondents. Sandy and Arlene receive AFDC and share expenses with the men with whom they live—men who are not the fathers of their children. Sandy is in a training program and Arlene is in college. Two other respondents, Jackie and Peggy, live with the father of their child. Like the men living with Sandy and Arlene, both fathers work full-time, but the respondents receive AFDC. Jackie is completing high school and Peggy is in junior college. Hattie, who lives with her son's father, and Krista, the only married respondent, have never received AFDC. Dee, Joyce, Robin, and Annie, all work except Annie, live with their mothers and receive no AFDC. Shelly receives no AFDC and lives with her aunt, supporting herself by working full-time. Annie, who is still completing high school, was very appreciative that her mother pays for her son's day care in addition to fully supporting them. Several respondents listed "getting off welfare" as one of their five-year goals. Ivy, who works half-time, saw the welfare check as belonging to her son, and it was her goal to get off AFDC as soon as possible.

Cher's story illustrates the difficult economic struggle facing young parents who have not completed their education and who work at low-wage jobs. A lack of money can contribute to the breakdown of already stressed relationships. Cher's father, an emotionally disabled veteran who had been a policemen before going into the army, died shortly before Cher's son was born. Her boyfriend had been close to Cher's father and got the idea of becoming a policeman from him. Cher describes the economic and emotional consequences of having too little money during her boyfriend's training period.

> It was hard for me 'cause he was gone most of time. The baby's situation, it was okay. I had my mother, my sisters, and everybody there to take care of him, *but the money situation—diapers, pampers, and food—became very tight. I didn't have no money to support myself. When I became nineteen, they cut me off of Social Security.* It was hard. I hated to ask my mother for money. She

knew I was cut off, so she was supporting me and the baby at the time. *He* [baby's father] *would send money home, but it just wasn't enough. So I had talked to him about going to get AFDC. He said no, 'cause he never wanted anybody he loved to be on that.* His mother was on it and he didn't want me to cope with the things she had to do. So I tried to be sneaky and go behind his back. One of my friends was with me and said, "Let's go try it." So I went up there and tried to sneak and lie and say I didn't know where he was. *Well, they caught him.* I gave them his middle name and last name, but no address, no other information. But on the computer, they matched his name to his address. He was totally upset with me. And that broke us up for about three months. He would come by and see the baby, but he wouldn't talk to me. That was hard for me, but after a while I learned to accept it, and I asked him if he wanted to break up. He said no. I said that was strange. He didn't want to be with me, but he wanted to be with the baby. He said, "I still love you, but I'm mad at what you did." I had to apologize. He said he didn't want me to go behind his back. He wanted me to be honest. We had to deal with that situation. AFDC wanted him to pay $185.00 a week, and I said $185.00 could help me pay my bills and buy us food for the house. That was costing us too much right there, we couldn't afford it. So I got off AFDC because they wanted him to pay too much child support. We made up after a while. It was real hard. His mother had gotten all into our personal business and said I didn't love him because I gave up his name, which I did not do. I didn't give up his name; I tried to do like my friends who went to school with me. They were getting AFDC and I figured, hey, I could be like them.

After this incident, Cher applied for Medicaid and subsidized housing. With these subsidies, for a while, she was able to rely on support from her son's father. Cher's story is a vivid example of the negative effect AFDC and child support enforcement can have on a father who is providing less support than AFDC would provide. That Cher's peers received AFDC without revealing the identities of the fathers of their children led her, when she was faced with financial difficulties, to imitate their behavior.

One often hears that teen mothers do not know the identity of the fathers of their children. Perhaps it is more accurate to assume that they choose not to reveal the father's name to public welfare agencies. While one can embrace the goal of making fathers financially responsible for their children, the effects of child support enforcement on relationships between young fathers with little job security and their families needs to be carefully studied. All of the thirty mothers I interviewed knew the identity of their babies' fathers. Sons were frequently named after their fathers, and fathers were present in places where they could easily be identified, such as in the delivery room at the birth of a child.

While the father of Cher's son has continued to support him, she reports that "things didn't work out right for us from that point on." In order to find a subsidized apartment, Cher, her mother, and son had to go to a predominantly white neighborhood far from her original neighborhood. Her boyfriend completed his police training and with his new commitment and her inconvenient location he has visited her less and less: "He had his uniform. He had his buddies. He had his job to love." He loved his job, but for Cher it was only a source of worry:

> I know he loves his job. I could not be a police officer's wife, dealing with him getting shot. *That scared me half to death, him being stabbed. I was frantic with worry about him and I couldn't deal with it. He was stabbed. It was a drug bust. He was shot in '87.* I said "I can't deal with this. You're here only half the time, and when your boss calls looking for you and I'm saying, 'I don't know where he is,' that frightens me to death." I couldn't deal with it so we decided to break it off for good.

Cher reported that she was back on AFDC and he was paying child support. She was pleased to have the $50 a month incentive welfare gives to mothers who are cooperative with the child support collection system. Cher is in her last year in high school and wants to go to college so that she can support herself and her son. She describes her relationship with her son's father as "just good friends."

I have told Cher's story in such detail because it illustrates so well the outer context of the lives of poor, urban, teenage mothers and young fathers. Cher had only one child and was an older teen completing her education, and the father of her child was committed to fulfilling his responsibilities. These characteristics place her in the group of teen parents not so "at risk" for poor educational and economic outcomes as are younger teens, teens with more than one child, and teen mothers who do not get support from the fathers of their children. Yet, economic pressures, housing, routine dependence on AFDC, and the violence of urban neighborhoods all conspired to increase the vulnerability of an already fragile relationship between two young unmarried parents.

Neighborhood

The majority of respondents live in the Roxbury and Dorchester neighborhoods of Boston. According to the City of Boston's *Roxbury and Dorchester Neighborhood Profiles,* in 1985 Roxbury was 75 percent black with significant numbers of low-income residents, mainly among minority families with children.[11] Single-parent households were overrepresented and Roxbury residents had a 31 percent poverty rate, compared to the citywide 21 percent poverty rate. One of the major changes in Roxbury over the past three decades has been its decline as a major manufacturing and retail center. As a result, the jobs in Roxbury in the eighties have been primarily service industry jobs.

Dorchester has a mixed racial profile. South Dorchester is 35 percent black, whereas North Dorchester is 18 percent black. Low-income residents were mainly found among minority families with children. Single-parent households were overrepresented and the poverty rate was 29 percent. Similarly, in North Dorchester, low-income residents were found mainly among minority families with children. The overall poverty rate in North Dorchester was 34 percent.

The young mothers are not isolated in these neighborhoods because there are a number who attend school and/or have working mothers or work themselves, but common community events and safe parks and recreational areas are missing from the neighborhoods. Several respondents live near Franklin Park, the largest park area in the central city. They reported that they do not use the park and warn neighborhood children not to go there because it is unsafe.

Consequently, children play in the street amid broken glass or in small, poorly equipped play areas in the housing projects. Some respondents are fond of roller skating, but the rink that they had frequented has become a meeting place for members of warring gangs, and skaters are frisked before being admitted.

Mothers reported "not going anywhere much" in the neighborhood. For most, parental responsibilities do not leave much time for activities or peer relationships. Some mothers fill their days with school and keeping clinic appointments for their children and for themselves.

Whereas Cher's fears, described above, of drugs and violence are a result of her child's father's choice to be a cop, others, like Peggy, feel the influence of drugs and violence on the streets where they live. Peggy lives in a well-kept, spacious apartment, but life beyond her door is not so attractive:

> I love having my son. I like to take care of him, spend time with him, and raise him. I see kids in the street. Their mothers don't care 'cause all they do is go around starting trouble, smoking, drinking beer, and stealing. So I have to spend time with him so he'll grow up not doing those things. The kids around here don't go to school much. All they do is stay around and smoke herb and stuff—even the little kids. The mothers don't send them to school. Because the mothers, all they do is smoke herb. I don't smoke and I don't drink. And the baby's father don't smoke or drink. So I don't let my son go out around here 'cause I don't want him to see them doing that stuff.

Unfortunately, Peggy had an even more direct experience with drugs and neighborhood violence. She let her eighteen-year-old brother come from down South to live with her. Peggy thought he would go to school in Boston because he had dropped out after ninth grade, but he did not attend. Instead he became involved with selling drugs and was stabbed in a dispute over money. A sixteen-year-old boy who was supposed to be his friend stabbed him ten times, and he nearly died. Peggy's mother took him back down South after he was released from a Boston hospital.

Linda, like Peggy, had the experience of a relative being stabbed in a drug transaction. For Linda's stepfather, the incident was fatal, whereas the violent and dramatic murder of the father of Ivy's baby involved alcohol rather than drugs:

> He got killed. He got murdered. A young boy around thirteen did it. It's the kind of life that these people want to lead. They want to go for bad. He got into a fight. One thing led to another and the next thing you know, he got killed. It was kind of sad because he was gone in five minutes. My son had just turned a year. We had a big birthday party for him in October and this happened maybe a week and a half after his birthday. It was like one week he was over here, and the next week he's gone. It was a big shock.
>
> He got killed in November. It happened on the street here. He was having trouble in school and at home. He came over to my house with his cousin, and I wasn't here. I was in school. I came home around 2:00 from school. He was in my house, and he had been drinking. He'd had a six-pack before he came by. He was totally drunk. "What are you doing over here drunk in front of my son? Come on, have some manners. I'll help you go home. I'll pay the cab, just go home." He was like, "Don't tell me what to do," and he was arguing. The neighbor downstairs got involved. She was telling him that my mother was not at home, and he should leave. He told her to mind her own business, and her son got involved. Next thing you know, his cousin got into it. They were fighting in the street, and the youngest boy grabbed a knife and while they were fighting, he stabbed him. He said he didn't mean to kill him. He just wanted to hurt him. And what made it so bad is that his [the boy who did the stabbing] mother was a Boston cop, and she was at the scene of the crime. Because it was her kid, she lost control. She was crying—she sat downstairs during the whole thing and cried. And I was yelling, "*Do Something!*"

Ivy lives on a side street off of a main street that runs through the heart of black Boston. It looked quiet and not dangerous. The housing consists of large frame multifamily dwellings in fair condition. The outward appearance of Ivy's street was better than the streets on which many respondents lived, particularly the five who reside in public housing. Similarly, the development where Peggy lives did not look dangerous from outward appearances, but a few weeks after I interviewed Peggy a teenager was gunned down just across the street from her apartment. He was killed in a drug dispute. While not all respondents have had such close encounters with violence, all are at risk of experiencing it. Violence in Boston's black neighborhoods is pervasive and often random. In the time since this study was completed, drug related violence and the murder rate in Boston, especially Roxbury, have increased. Neighborhood safety and police practices regarding young black males have become major political issues in Boston

Community Organizations

Over and over the response was "no" to the question "Are you associated with any organizations (including the church) in your community?" The church in the black community has historically been a strong neighborhood institution that has sustained many families through hardship. Therefore, I was surprised that so few respondents were associated with a church. Some reported occasional church attendance, and several stated the intention to have their child(ren) christened. Most respondents reported no church affiliation. Others reported that they had been active in the past but no longer attended church. For example, Peggy reported that everyone had gone to church when her grandmother had lived in Boston, but when she moved down South, everyone stopped going.

Arlene reported that she did not go to church because the new father at the Catholic church she once attended refused to christen her son: "He told me 'I don't think your child is going to grow up as a true Christian because you don't go to church.' And I said, 'What?' And that was the end of that." Arlene has not gone back to church since this incident. Fortunately for Arlene, this rebuff from the priest was balanced by positive contacts with other professionals. Although other respondents did not report being rejected by churches, Mae's experience indicates that unmarried mothers may feel uncomfortable returning to church. Mae did not feel comfortable returning to the traditional black church where she had met the father of her two children. She stated the reasons she stopped going: "I don't feel like it. I feel it's wrong to go to church or I feel that you should follow right what God says and not do your own thing. If you want to do your own thing, stay outside the church. See, I feel like I've been doing my own thing. I've been doing things that ain't approved by God's laws. I know that."

At one time, Mae's boyfriend's church and her mother's church where Mae sang solos in the choir played an important role in her life. Her evaluation that she was living an unacceptable life-style was probably influenced by the strong disapproval of her boyfriend's mother, a church member who was upset by Mae's first pregnancy and advised her to terminate the second pregnancy, which occurred when the first baby was only nine months old. Mae felt that there was wide social distance between her and her boyfriend, whom she described as middle-class. Mae lived in the housing project where she was born. Her father, an alcoholic, had not married her mother, and each of Mae's four sisters had babies out of wedlock. Ironically, Mae reported that her boyfriend had assured her that he "would not get me pregnant, and I believed him. I thought he had control over his body." Mae's wish to avoid her boyfriend's mother and her friends and her feeling that she was not living an exemplary life kept her away from the church, a potentially supportive community. Mae reported no other involvement with neighborhood organizations.

In contrast, when the church rebuffed Arlene, she found help from the staff at the neighborhood health center where she participated in a parenting group. The health center was located in the housing project where Arlene had grown up and had served as her family's primary health care facility. Arlene had not lived in the project for several years, but she returned to the center for the parenting program. Respondents were not active in other voluntary associations such as the YWCA or settlement houses.

In Liz's case, a lack of knowledge about community resources could have deprived her from pursuing a long-standing interest: Liz wants to be "in TV." By this she means television acting. She recalled reading scripts in school and liking it very much: "All my life I've wanted to be in TV acting. TV is interesting to me. I know if it's something you want to do, if you put your mind to it, you can do it." Liz referred to an acting school located downtown but was suspicious about its reputation. I asked Liz if she had heard of the Elma Lewis School of Fine Arts, a well-known Afro-American arts school located a few blocks from where she grew up. She had never heard of the school and knew nothing about its activities.

Limited knowledge about community resources, a lack ⟨
to programs, the absence of programs, or insensitive prof⟨⟨⟨
played a part in some respondents' limited relationships to institutions. The availability of caring adults outside the family is particularly necessary to the development of adolescents from poor
single-parent families if they are to overcome many of the disadvantages that confront them.

Community Role Models

One of the characteristics of the study respondents is their limited
involvement with adults outside the family. When asked about
influential persons in their lives, respondents did not name teachers
or other community figures.

One respondent, Ivy, thought that the teachers she knew, except
for one, did not know how to relate to inner-city students and had
a poor opinion of them:

> You don't take somebody from Lexington [a suburb of Boston]
> and stick them in Dorchester High or West Roxbury High and tell
> the students they know what it's like. They don't. They think that
> all city kids are troublemakers, and a lot of them are not. A lot of
> them want understanding and they don't know how to get it. They
> don't understand that you can't really get through to a teacher.
> They have enough problems of their own, and they don't want to
> hear yours. I think there ought to be a program in the school
> system that you can get credit for by going there and saying it like
> it is. We had one good-looking teacher—very stylish. He walked
> in and said, "What's up?" He would be sitting in the chair back-
> wards. He was a normal teacher. He told us we were going to talk
> about what's happening today. Today is history. But he's not there
> any more.

Ivy was the only respondent to mention a teacher, except for
Corrie, who told me about a teacher who had spat on her because
he always "sprayed" when he talked. When Corrie, eleven at the
time, insisted that he apologize to her, the teacher refused. She hit
him and was expelled. Corrie was allowed to return to school only

after her mother interceded and Corrie agreed to sit in the back of the room for the remainder of the school year.

Only one respondent, Sandy, identified professional women outside the family as role models: a social worker in the adolescent clinic at Brigham and Women's Hospital whom she had met during her first pregnancy, a social worker in a shelter, and a woman who volunteered to be Sandy's big sister. Sandy assessed the importance of the hospital social worker in this way:

> There are a lot of reasons why I changed. I would say I did 90 percent of it myself. But the 10 percent was the social workers I did like enough to talk to and get feedback that was helpful. If I didn't like one, I didn't give her enough information for her to determine what was going on. With Patricia, I told her everything, and she took it all so positively. That helped to establish what we have now, and she'll just be one of those people I can always go back to. And in the shelter I had a wonderful social worker who was somebody like Patricia, who noticed that regardless of the things I did in the past, that I was really a good person, you know what I'm saying?

When Sandy moved out of the city, she told Patricia that she felt lonely and isolated. Patricia arranged for Sandy to have a big sister. Of her big sister, Sandy said:

> Oh, I love her, I love her. She's like forty-seven years old and she's great! I love her. I just always liked older women, an older woman that's successful anyway. *I always like to talk to them because if they like me, they're going to want to show me that I have potential to be successful.* My big sister just makes me feel so good! We can go out to dinner and drinks and have a real intellectual conversation, you know. She's young at heart. She's not real strict, like "You're only nineteen." She just looks at me like a woman. She's a vice-president in a company. She just got the job five months ago. She's unreal!

Sandy's big sister and the social workers whom she admires are nonjudgmental about Sandy's past. They accept Sandy as she is. They view her as an adult with worth and potential. Yet Sandy's experience with professionals has not always been positive:

I had a social worker from the department of social services who hated her job and no one in her department knew it except me, because I was one of her clients. I could see how she dealt with me so I could detect that she just did not like her job, and that's why I didn't meet with her. If I had an appointment to meet with her, I never even showed up. Because I said, "Why am I gonna take an hour out of my time to tell somebody how I'm feeling when they really don't care?" It's hard to pull out your feelings, you know, and to have to waste them. She used to jog in the middle of the day for her lunch hour. If I needed anything during that time, "Well, I'm sorry I'm gonna be jogging from one to two. So why don't you give me a call around 3:30? I should be in." Okay, I would just be home 'til 3:30. "You just take your time and you just get back to me when you're done." That's my attitude. That's how it's supposed to be.

This social worker did not practice the elementary lesson of communicating that the client's concerns take precedence over the worker's convenience. Fortunately, by the time Sandy met the social worker described above, she had had several years of experience with institutions and individual professionals. She can remember the exact date she met Patricia at Brigham and Women's Hospital, because this meeting followed a most traumatic experience for Sandy:

February 22, 1984. That date sticks in my head. Not only was it my first prenatal appointment, *but the day I got out of the mental hospital.* That was a horrible experience, because I am not crazy, and that is a place for crazy people. You know it's okay for outpatients, but being an inpatient in there is terrible. 'Cause I was in there with all the nuts—people who were at the point of drooling on themselves. Just because they wanted an evaluation of where my head was at. It turned out my head wasn't really as messed up as they thought it was. *They thought I was crazy for making the decision to have a baby in my situation. Why was I trying to bring a baby into the world when I wasn't stable?* The judge ordered me to be committed for an evaluation. I was involved with the court because of my grand larceny. Luckily, I was there only two weeks, because I believe what scared me about that was for people who get committed in my situation for longer than two weeks. That place could make you crazy! Because I was nothing but depressed the whole time I was there.

Sandy's story illustrates that teenagers perceive the procedures in place to protect pregnant teens who are thought to be depressed or suicidal as terrifying and not helpful. It is fortunate that following such a negative encounter in a mental health facility, Sandy's social worker and the hospital adolescent pregnancy clinic provided positive institutional connections and positive professional role models. It is hard to imagine a middle-class teenager ending up in a mental institution to determine her mental fitness for motherhood. Sandy's resilience, hope, and humor about her past experiences are attributable to her inner strength and the positive involvement of the hospital social worker and Sandy's big sister.

Sandy, however, was an exception. Although professional and community role models were in short supply for most of the mothers, teen parents were in abundant supply in their schools and neighborhoods. For example, Annie, who became pregnant at fourteen, knew at least ten teenagers who were mothers. Annie did not think of these girls as "best friends": "Some of them didn't go to school with me. They lived around the area I live in, but we would get together." Agnes reported that she had four friends who had babies. Robbie was hesitant to give a number. She reported "all" of her friends were teen mothers.

Arlene was the only respondent who reported the loss of a friendship because she was pregnant: "One of my closest friends just left the friendship, just like that. We had been friends since ninth grade and this was in the twelfth." Some respondents reported that they were the first girl to become pregnant, whereas others knew many girls who had been pregnant before they were. Respondents' reports and my own observations led me to conclude that teenage childbearing was common in the neighborhoods where respondents lived. On one occasion, I interviewed a respondent at a neighborhood health center, and the waiting room was filled with teen mothers and their children. Thus, while health centers in respondents' neighborhoods are positive places for health care and counseling, they, like the homes of teen mothers, also illustrate that teen childbearing is a common occurrence among urban black females.

8
Findings,
Research Implications,
and Policy Suggestions

There is no lack of explanations for the occurrence of pregnancy among black teen women. Prominent among the explanations are early sexual activity and the lack of consistent birth control use. Both excuses are well documented but are not sufficient explanations of why more pregnant girls do not choose to have abortions or put their babies up for adoption, or why they want babies in the first place.

The experience of becoming pregnant prior to marriage is not unusual; consequently, the present-day concern is not simply a question of premarital pregnancy. What is disturbing is the occurrence of another factor, namely, that many pregnant girls exhibit no shame, have babies, keep them, and do not get married. For pregnancy not to carry the expectation of marriage is a fairly recent phenomenon. This new development is not easy to understand. Sex seems to most persons to be something that suggests a continuing relationship, and marriage is one way of continuing that relationship. Some popular explanations advanced are easy access to welfare, the removal of the stigma associated with unmarried motherhood, and the increase in female-headed households. These explanations no doubt do account for the actions of some teenagers, but it is difficult to imagine that they convey the entire story.

It was the need to know more about the motivations of teenage mothers that prompted this study and its method. Teenage mothers are often categorized as "children having children." The phrase itself suggests that the persons involved are immature and not able to fully understand their own actions. This interpretation causes many to dismiss the teenage mother as a reliable source of knowledge about the uncoupling of pregnancy and marriage. I think this attitude is a mistake. In spite of their youth and in some instances immaturity, listening to teenage mothers can provide insight and truth.

Ethnographic research, unlike large data sets, when specifically designed to study teenage childbearing will overcome some of the problems of previous research, such as the exclusion of the teenage mother's perspective. Greater knowledge of the teen mother's family life, peers, and relation to neighborhood institutions can better inform us of what having babies and keeping them means to the teenager.

Findings

Primary socialization of the respondents occurs in families where the mother had also been a teenage mother. The consistent adult role model in the lives of the thirty young mothers is the girl's own mother, who not only began childbearing when she was a teenager but also had children by different fathers and never married. Thus the respondents learned that childbearing is an acceptable, possibly even an expected career.

The acceptability of early childbearing is further reinforced by the examples of sisters, cousins, aunts, and peers. Therefore, teen childbearing for the respondents represents the repetition of a familiar pattern that is expressed in the childbearing behavior of their female role models.

No single pattern describes the relation between the thirty young mothers' relationship with their own fathers and the girls' relationship with the young men who are the fathers of their children. Both relationships were tenuous. Fewer than a third of the respondents have contact with their own fathers, and about half have contact with their child(ren)'s father(s). Three mothers with one child live with the father of that child, whereas none of the mothers of two children lives with the father of either of her children. The dominant pattern for respondents' fathers and the fathers of the respondents' children was that fathers did not establish themselves as legal (by marriage), economic, or sociological fathers.

Few respondents expected to marry the father of their child. Marriage was not as important to the young mothers as completing high school and living independently, which were frequently mentioned goals some hoped to achieve in the near future. A few aspired to marry and agreed that having a father present made for a more "complete" family. Some thought that a relationship with the father was important but that a mother and her children were a "complete" family. Still others reported that they did not wish to marry the father because he was immature, although the father and his family wanted the marriage. Some of the respondents felt they were too young to marry and that marriage imposed more restrictions on personal freedom than did motherhood.

One may raise the question of whether or not early childbearing with little concern for marriage is a result of the socialization process or a more deeply embedded cultural pattern. I see the two rationales as related. These daughters were not socialized to have babies in the sense that their mothers explicitly told them to get pregnant or not to marry, but if one considers the socialization process as occurring through implicit as well as explicit messages— or do as I do, not as I say—these teens are indeed socialized to motherhood. Further, as argued in the preceding chapters, while teen childbearing occurs among black teens in numbers disproportionate to their numbers in the population, white teens in the United States in comparison with teens in other Western countries also have disproportionately high rates of pregnancy, abortion, and birth. Therefore, the "cultural" influences go beyond family role models and the black subculture.

For example, "Single mothers: Making it their way" appeared in the *New York Times* on Thursday, January 12, 1989, and a few weeks later, the *Boston Globe's* feature centerpiece was titled "Gay couples begin a baby boom."[12] These articles are indicative of the existence of subcultures in the United States that do not hold to the norms that traditional marriage precedes childbearing or that a sociological father need be male. While the norm of legitimacy is still present in the total society, for some upper middle class women, white and black, for members of avant garde groups, lesbians, and some lower-class blacks and whites, these norms have lost much of their saliency. Our society is caught between old and new paradigms of what constitutes a family and who can perform the tasks associated with parental roles.

Thus the larger culture has removed the stigma previously associated with unwed motherhood. Unmarried mothers are no longer isolated, so there is less chance that they will be stigmatized. Consequently, reproductive behavior that was once more exclusively associated with blacks and the lower class now occurs among non-minority and middle-class groups in the society. Because blacks have always had higher rates of illegitimacy and higher poverty rates than whites, the accepting attitude in the larger culture toward single mothers may make black adolescents more vulnerable than others to increased out-of-wedlock births.

The young women I spoke with think of themselves as responsible mothers. I found that the majority of them have adequate parental conceptions and are able to understand the needs of their children while attempting to meet their own needs. They do not view early childbearing as having ruined their lives, and they see themselves, like their mothers, as capable of rearing children without marriage or a commitment from the father. Few of them expect to marry and nearly all want at least one other child. Their early childbearing and the early childbearing of their mother has led them to believe that one is "too old" to have children much beyond the age of thirty. Consequently, several respondents want to be finished with childbearing by the time they are twenty-five. Such feelings are further evidence of how family patterns influence the thinking of these young mothers. Considering that these respondents were born when their mothers were teenagers and their mothers have become grandmothers before the age of forty, it is understandable that age thirty may be considered "too old" for childbearing. This perception holds for the urban black teens, whereas professional women adopt the opposite view—they want to postpone having children until after age thirty, when their careers will be well established.

The lives of my thirty respondents span the 1970s and 1980s, a decade marked by school busing, racial unrest, white flight, declining job opportunities, and the weakening of traditional community institutions. Most respondents lived in Roxbury and Dorchester, Boston's predominantly black neighborhoods, which are poor inner-city communities marked by urban decay.

Poverty has long been associated with family disintegration and out-of-wedlock births. The sociologist E. Franklin Frazier, who for over four decades was considered the foremost authority on the black family, argued that the high incidence of out-of-wedlock births was a function of postemancipation social and economic forces at work in the rural South. He said that black motherhood was "free on the whole from institutional and communal control" (Frazier, 1966: 88). This lack of control followed the black to the North, where in the midst of urban poverty and disorganization, unmarried motherhood continued to flourish.

Frazier's argument, put forth in the late forties, is similar in conclusion to the argument made by contemporary sociologist William J. Wilson (1987). Wilson argues that the structure of today's poor, urban black family is primarily influenced by economic conditions created by declining wages and joblessness among young black males. Joblessness, incarceration, and high mortality rates among black males create a shrinking pool of marriageable black men and provide no incentive for young black women to delay childbearing. The dispersal of the black middle class from the inner city to suburban neighborhoods contributes to social disorganization, the decline in the support of neighborhood institutions, and the lack of role models for black children. Wilson's argument is compelling and offers an explanation for the outer forces that influence decision making about the most personal aspects of life—childbearing and marriage.

The relation between economic status, employability of black males, and marriage is difficult to disentangle. These variables are but one illustration of the complexity of the outer context of teen mothers lives. Wilson's contention that black male unemployment is the major cause of unwed motherhood among blacks may be an overstatement of the case. As stated earlier, some mothers are socialized to single parenthood. Among some other mothers, the earning capacity of the males has had an impact on their relationship as Cher's story illustrates. But because marriage expectations are based on a host of factors, including experience in one's family of origin and cultural expectations, more evidence is needed before one could call unemployment the major cause of the low marriage rate of black males. One needs to take into consideration the impact of the acceptance of alternative family configurations by black males and females.

This study confirms the relationship between poverty and unmarried motherhood. Receiving AFDC, although seldom the sole source of income, is indicative of the poverty status of the mother. Although twenty-three of the respondents reported AFDC as a source of income, only four respondents reported AFDC as the only source of income. Five respondents work full-time, and one works half-time. Two respondents receive formal child support payments, whereas fourteen fathers make informal financial contributions or provide other material support. These young mothers do not fit the terms "welfare dependent" or "underclass." They rely heavily, but not solely, on welfare. That most respondents live with their mothers means that housing, an expensive and scarce commodity in Boston, is an important "in-kind" (non-cash, i.e., housing, surplus food, or medicaid) benefit. Respondents recognized this and mentioned housing in a list of support from their mothers. Although I have suggested that these families cannot accurately be described as welfare dependent or "underclass," that so many of them are eligible for AFDC, even with a working mother, indicates that some of the respondents' families are among the working poor.

Respondents' description of jobs held by the fathers of their children led me to conclude that the jobs provided little security and were not high-wage jobs. Economic forces in present-day black inner-city neighborhoods may have an effect on the incidence of out-of-wedlock childbearing among black teen women that is similar to postemancipation economic forces. Several respondents reported that their child(ren)'s father and his family want them to marry. Their reasons for postponing marriage were not economic. Wanting to be independent like their mothers, the father lacking maturity, and the women believing that they did not need a husband to help with child rearing or to make a "complete" family were among the mothers' explanations for not getting married.

Although these findings do not negate Frazier's or Wilson's argument, they do suggest that many factors other than the joblessness of black males and the shrinking of the pool of marriageable men influence black teen mothers not to aspire to marriage. Talking to the young mothers elicits a much more complex set of attitudes and expectations regarding marriage. Among them is a belief that they, like their mothers, can rear children without a man. In their experience, dependable emotional bonds are made between mothers and their children, not between children and their fathers or women and the fathers of their children.

Instead of unemployment or a missing pool of men, socialization was the pervasive factor in the lives of these thirty young mothers: they had been socialized into the childbearing and marriage patterns of their mothers and sisters. Having children during the teen years and without marriage may be a variant life-style that is now institutionalized among low-income, black, single-parent households. Schools and neighborhood institutions have not provided these teens with professional role models, information about life options, or sufficient self-affirming experiences to influence them not to become parents.

Conspicuously missing from respondents' experiences were influential teachers and positive feelings about the public schools they had attended. During their pregnancies, at least half of the respondents had attended school at St. Mary's Home at St. Margaret's Hospital or the Crittenton Hastings House. These maternity schools were fondly referred to by respondents as "pregnant school." Most contrasted their positive school experience in "pregnant school" with an unhappy public school experience. For positive connections to institutions, then, these respondents looked to the health care system and maternity schools. Their experiences with both of these institutions are intertwined with pregnancy and the birth experience. Thus, in a subtle way, for these young women pregnancy brought care and attention that had been lacking in their school careers and in neighborhood institutions.

Few respondents are related to churches or neighborhood organizations, instead health care institutions had regular contact with respondents. Relationships to hospitals and neighborhood health centers, together with good health and early prenatal care, may account for the fact that only two out of the forty-five babies born to respondents were low birth weight. But, contact with the health care system had not resulted in diligent birth control use by most respondents. Some mothers reported irregular contraceptive use even after having two babies. Having a second child meant continued contact with health care institutions and less contact with schools.

Of the thirty mothers, eleven were school dropouts. Of the eleven, nine had two children. By comparison, only two mothers with one child were dropouts, and they worked full-time. Thirteen mothers with one child were in school or were high school graduates, and two among them were enrolled in college. This marked difference in educational attainment between the two groups of mothers confirms findings from other studies that rapid repeat births (births within two years of each other) delay return to school and sometimes impede it altogether.

My respondents' median self-esteem score was 52, the same as the median score for teen mothers from three major cities in the 1979 CWLA study (Miller, 1983). That study included 127 teen mothers age sixteen and younger. Of the 127, 85 percent were black. According to Miller (1983), who developed the self-esteem questionnaire from Rosenberg's and Coopersmith's reliable scales, 52 is a relatively high score. A comparison of the self-esteem scores of the nineteen women who have completed or were enrolled in school with those of the eleven dropouts showed a positive relationship between education and self-esteem. The relationship proved to be statistically significant at the .0058 level. The mean score for the nineteen enrolled in school was 54.3, whereas the eleven dropouts had a mean score of 48.5. Consequently, high-quality educational institutions at the neighborhood level from early childhood throughout the educational careers of low-income minority children are crucial for achievement and the development of positive self-esteem.

Fourteen of the women identified having a baby as an event that made them feel good about themselves. Seven reported work or other kinds of events such as getting a driver's license or having the father of the baby agree to stay after the baby was born, whereas six reported that an educational event had made them feel great about themselves. These findings suggest that experiences that make teens feel competent should be widely available at home, in the school, and in community institutions.

All respondents thought that at least completing high school was not only desirable, but necessary for obtaining a job and for being able to help their children with school work. In spite of these positive attitudes about education, the school as an institution was not regarded as supportive to respondents. In fact, school busing within the city of Boston and voluntary busing to suburban schools resulted in the loss of neighborhood schools as supportive institutions. Although suburban schools provided educational opportunity, busing caused some respondents to be cut off from the neighborhood and made the school inaccessible to parents.

Research Implications

This study shows what rich insights can come from "children who have children." It is imperative that we listen more attentively to them. With the exception of Ladner (1972) and Stack (1974), most of the ethnographic literature on the culture of black inner-city neighborhoods focuses on male subjects (Liebow, 1967; Anderson, 1978; MacLeod, 1987). The males in these studies are portrayed as having loose family ties and being jobless or having sporadic work lives. It is now time to explore these issues with young women.

Research of the last decade and a half has sketched a large picture of teenage pregnancy. Small-scale, in-depth studies are now needed to shift the emphasis from the focus on adverse outcomes that has dominated the literature on teenage pregnancy and parenting to a search for possible causes of the behavior of teenagers and for the incentives that lead them to choose teenage motherhood. Such studies will assist in the effort to understand the differential effects of early childbearing on teens from similar backgrounds. More study is needed of the supports and characteristics that allow for "recovery" from early childbearing.

To increase the life options of poor and minority teenagers, it is first necessary to gain a better understanding of the teen mother's perspective on her own life and her future. While adverse outcomes of early childbearing show up in studies of teenage mothers, too little attention has been paid to the conditions that precede pregnancy. For example, teenage girls often drop out of school because they are pregnant. Yet, some respondents had welcomed pregnancy as a good excuse to leave a disorderly, unfriendly school experience.

An absence of after-school neighborhood recreational programs for preteen children and too few alternative childcare resources for working mothers are characteristic of the urban neighborhoods where respondents live. We do not know why some teens exposed to these conditions do not become mothers while others do. Ethnographic studies of teens from similar backgrounds who do not become mothers are needed to tell us if having a baby is "risking the future." *Do poor, black teens who do not become mothers enter the primary labor market, go to college, and have lives appreciably different from those who do become mothers?* This outcome is sometimes implied. Only comparative research between those who do and do not become teen mothers will tell us if this is so. Such studies should be carried out in many locations and with samples of varying sizes. With larger samples and a combination of qualitative and quantitative approaches, it should be possible to uncover the different paths followed by teen mothers as well as consistent patterns in subjects' experiences. It is natural for researchers to identify patterns and look for similarities in the population under study. This tendency masks the complexity of teen childbearing. Although we can identify the similarities in economic circumstances and family structure in young mothers, their individual ways of coping are easily submerged by generalizations.

Furstenberg, Brooks-Gunn, and Morgan's (1987) longitudinal research based on a 1960s Baltimore study shows that examining the lives of teenage mothers immediately following and shortly after they give birth may lead to an emphasis on adverse effects. For example, seventeen years after their original research the researchers found that many mothers had had spells on welfare, but that they had not been long-term welfare dependents. The majority of the women in the study, although not doing as well economically as those who were not teen childbearers, were working and self-sufficient. Based on these findings, Furstenberg believes that the adverse effects of early childbearing may have been overstated.

More longitudinal follow-up studies of teenage program participants need to be done to give perspective to reports on the effects of early childbearing. Studies such as this one should be followed up and expanded to include perspectives of teen fathers and respondents' mothers. Research that includes the mothers of teenage mothers may lead to a better understanding of the socialization process within the family.

Policy Implications

At the heart of the decline in inner-city neighborhoods is a weakening of community institutions. Wilson (1987) argues that the flight of middle-class blacks from the inner city has removed the source of leadership and financial support for schools, churches, and social agencies. Married working couples had not only supported community institutions but had also provided role models for children from one-parent welfare families. The flight of the middle class occurred at the same time as school busing and the withdrawal of federal money from urban areas.

My respondents' poverty of relationships with schools and churches and lack of identification with adult role models outside of the home is, I believe, related to Wilson's observations that the exodus of the black middle class from the inner city has weakened institutions and removed positive role models. What policies and programs are realistic in the face of such urban decline? It is unlikely that the decline in black neighborhoods will subside given the lack of federal investment in our central cities. Moreover, urban violence is likely to increase working- and middle-class flight. Greater investment from the federal government in urban housing, schools, and recreational facilities can make a difference in the lives of poor families and encourage middle-class blacks to remain. Perhaps even some white people and businesses will then return to the city. State government and local school committees, even with shrinking revenues, can reorder priorities to make elementary schools places that give children a solid education and a vision of the future.

The kinds of programs reviewed by Schorr (1988) in *Within Our Reach* would go a long way toward improving the lives of poor and working-poor teenagers and single parents in the inner city. She reviews comprehensive programs across the country that have made a difference in the lives of poor and vulnerable children. An essential

ingredient in these programs is committed professionals who serve
as role models for young people. Of particular interest are school
programs that work, such as Dr. James Comer's experiment in the
New Haven Public Schools. Comer's program for changing the cli-
mate of schools in poor neighborhoods rested on the principle of
disciplined school management, adjunct teams of mental health professionals to provide services to pupils and consultation to teachers,
and parent participation in school governance. Started in 1968, the
programs have been in effect long enough to test the efficacy of the
model. The socioeconomic status of the children has not changed,
but attendance, behavior, and achievement scores have changed in a
positive direction in the experimental schools.

Programs based on Comer's model are now being replicated in
other New Haven schools and schools around the country. Local
school committees have the power to allocate resources to such
programs. According to an article announcing a Rockefeller Foundation $15 million dollar grant to expand Comer's program, the
program has already been adopted by more than seventy schools.[13]
The success of Comer's programs in raising achievement scores and
lowering dropout and teen pregnancy rates argues for the support of
policies and programs that help schools achieve their central pur-
poses of education and socialization. These programs seem particularly relevant because girls who repeat a grade early in their school
careers are at higher risk for teen pregnancy.

In addition to policies to assist schools in achieving their mis-
sion, recreation and after-school programs should be made available
to preschool children and continue through adolescence. The respondents in my study did not receive regular attention from schools or
community agencies until they were pregnant. Then health care
agencies and "pregnant schools" concentrated on making them and
their babies healthy and on teaching parenting skills. These efforts
should be continued for girls who do become pregnant, but to prevent teenage pregnancy, we need programs that pay attention to
children before, rather than after, they are in trouble. Mae, one of
my thirty mothers, stated the case for prevention: "I feel that people
slack up more on you if you're not in need. My mother always told
me something. She said, 'They help the sick people in the world, not
the healthy, not the people that are healthy-minded.' And I find it to

be true. See, like my father, he gets a lot of attention because he's an alcoholic. But he doesn't want to stop his alcoholism. People give him free this, free that, free TV, free apartment."

Mae has learned that there are secondary gains from dysfunctional behavior. She identifies a dilemma of the service system: how to help without fostering dependency or encouraging the behavior to continue. The answer to this dilemma may not be known. There is evidence that small, coherent, and nonbureaucratic programs offer positive support and help prevent outcomes such as school dropout and teen pregnancy (Schorr, 1988).

Ivy has stated that hot lines for teenagers are no replacement for interested adults and personal contact. "You don't want a telephone. People are not there—it's not a good option." Good options for teenagers should be introduced long before the teen years. Caring adult role models from early childhood through high school will inform girls that becoming a mother is not their only avenue to fulfillment and recognition.

Furstenberg, Brooks-Gunn, and Morgan (1987: 153) suggest that education, job training, and stable job opportunities for disadvantaged males are as important as programs for teenage mothers. In addition, programs designed for parents of teen mothers and for the teen mothers' children may broaden the socialization experiences of inner-city children and break the cycle of teenage childbearing.

Finally, the thirty young mothers in this study see their lives as enriched by childbearing. In spite of poor schools and little contact with churches and neighborhood organizations, these mothers have relatively high self-esteem, which has been enhanced by having children. They are poor but not without hope. They live in impoverished neighborhoods but are not impoverished by them. Their children have begun life with a healthy start. The challenge is to sustain this beginning by providing educational and recreational programs to assure that these children have the support and attention from community institutions that were missing from their mothers' lives. We then may be preparing the future generation for enriched, not merely acceptable lives.

Appendix A: Background on This Study

Massachusetts Adolescent Pregnant and Parenting System

My sample of thirty black teen mothers was identified through the Massachusetts Adolescent Pregnant and Parenting System (MAPPS). The majority of the young mothers gave birth at Brigham and Women's and St. Margaret's Hospitals in Boston. Crittenton Hastings House, The Young Parents Program at Children's Hospital, and the Whittier Street, Dimock, and Roxbury Comprehensive Neighborhood Health Centers were sources for study participants. With the exception of Crittenton Hastings House, these sources are hospitals and neighborhood health centers.

The Massachusetts Department of Public Health collects standardized data from programs that serve the health needs of pregnant and parenting teens, which are funded by its Division of Family Health Services. The Massachusetts Adolescent Pregnant and Parenting System (MAPPS) is a statewide monitoring system based on the Impact Evaluation Model used by the Too-Early-Childbearing Network programs, which are funded by the Mott Foundation. The MAPPS data collection system began in 1982 and includes approximately ten programs located at twenty-seven sites across the state. These programs annually serve approximately fifteen hundred adolescents eighteen years of age or younger, who have not completed high school. MAPPS collects information on age, ethnicity, number of previous pregnancies, birth control use, marital status, household composition, living arrangements, mobility, and educational status at the initial screening interview. At birth and six, twelve, eighteen, and twenty-four months after delivery, information is collected on sociodemographic variables, educational status, relationship to the baby's father, employment status, supplementary income sources, pregnancy history, substance use, prenatal care information, services received, birth outcomes, repeat pregnancies, and subsequent births.

The MAPPS data was especially helpful in identifying a group of Boston black teenage women with first and second births. Professionals in the Division of Family Health Services receive, computerize, and analyze the data from all sites. They freely welcome researchers from outside the department who wish to make use of their findings; if research requires access to individual MAPPS clients, as mine did, the division refers researchers directly to the data collection sites. Of the Boston MAPPS data collection sites, Brigham and Women's Hospital Consortium for Pregnant and Parenting Teens and St. Margaret's Hospital were selected because 57 percent of the approximately seven hundred black MAPPS clients seen in Boston between 1982 and 1986 were served in these two settings; it seemed likely that a sample selected from the population of black teens whose babies were born at either of these two institutions would meet the study criteria.

Sample Selection

In December 1986 I selected identification numbers of potential study respondents from a MAPPS computer list provided by the Division of Family Health Services; this list was comprised of Boston black teens who were receiving health care at either of the two hospitals. (Names and addresses of potential subjects were available only from the hospitals). I chose Identification numbers from the MAPPS computer listing of teens who were pregnant for a second time at up to twenty-four months follow-up. The director of the Consortium for Pregnant and Parenting Teens, who is responsible for MAPPS data collection at Brigham and Women's Hospital, provided access to data collection forms so that I was able to match names with identification numbers. The associate director of social services and the director of the Adolescent Clinic at Brigham and Women's, and the director of Family Life Services at St. Margaret's, assisted in the identification of participants and helped in the human-subjects review process.

A different procedure was used at each hospital to allow me access to information about the resolution of pregnancies. At St. Margaret's, the director of Family Life Services gave me the information and told potential respondents about the study; at Brigham and Women's Hospital, I was given access to a log book in which social workers had recorded pregnancy outcome, the name of the social worker, and whether or not the teen was lost to follow-up, had moved, or was receiving services in another hospital or program. When this procedure failed to produce fifteen mothers, social workers identified teens due to deliver second babies who had not shown up in the MAPPS data because of lag time between when the hospital submitted data to the Department of Public Health and when it was entered in the computer. Relying on the computer printout meant that some potential subjects were missed. Direct referrals from hospital social workers, contact with additional agencies, and respondents from the MAPPS list were the sources for subjects with second births.

Similar steps were taken to select fifteen potential interviewees with one birth. MAPPS data was used to identify such teens who were similar in age to those with two births. The birth dates of the first babies of *all* members of the sample (both the teen mothers with one child and those with two children) correspond as closely as possible. I wanted to assure that the mothers of one child had had a similar amount of time to get pregnant a second time as those who had two children. Three possible matches from the pool of teens with one child were chosen for each subject in the group with two births.

Problems Encountered in Sample Selection

In 1985, according to statistics from the Massachusetts Department of Public Health, of the 6,857 births to teenagers fifteen to nineteen years of age, 1,130 (16 percent) were second or third births. Of these, 216 (or 19 percent) were to black teens. The percent of all teens in MAPPS with second or higher births is even smaller. For example, between 1982 and 1984, 192 black teens out of a total of 743 in MAPPS included only three (1.5 percent) second or repeat births compared to none for white teens (Gorbach, Walker, Klein, and RuchRoss, 1986). A computer listing of births to black MAPPS clients between 1982 and 1986 recorded only eleven second births at the two hospitals from which my sample was chosen. Surprisingly, the social workers anticipated no difficulty in locating fifteen mothers with two children. One explanation for this may be the disappointment each social worker feels when one of her clients returns to the hospital pregnant again. This sense of failure and the fact that not all second pregnancies ended in birth may have made the number of second births seem higher than they actually were to social workers.

While the selection of teens with two children required referrals from other agencies to make the sample large enough, they were easily contacted once they were identified because the two-year follow-up period had not ended. In contrast, teens with one child born around the same time as the first child of a mother with two children had often completed follow-up and were no longer in touch with the social workers. This meant that the last recorded address may have changed since they were in contact with the hospital. Altogether, the major problem in the selection of mothers with two children was getting a sufficient number, while the major difficulty in selecting the mothers of one child was locating them.

The original criterion for the study called for a sample of persons aged seventeen or younger; however, two eighteen-year-old mothers are included. To get fifteen mothers with two children, I included one eighteen-year-old mother who had two children before her twentieth birthday. I then included in the sample of mothers with one child an eighteen-year-old who had given birth close to the time that the other eighteen-year-old mother had her first child.

Contacting Subjects

After matching respondents' identification numbers to names, the names were given to the social workers. Social workers informed potential interviewees that I was conducting a study with young mothers to learn about their ideas and feelings on pregnancy, birth, and motherhood. They were told that interviews could occur in a place of their choosing. If the mother agreed to participate in the study, the social worker secured permission to release the respondent's telephone number. In the few instances where respondents had no telephone, they were encouraged by hospital social workers to call the interviewer. Interview times were set up by phone except in two cases where the interviewer went directly to the homes of respondents after failing to make contact by letter.

Protection of Human Subjects

I submitted an application to the Committee for the Protection of Human Subjects from Research Risk requesting permission to involve patients from the Adolescent Reproductive Health Service at Brigham and Women's Hospital. The application explains the goals of the study, outlines the process for obtaining informed consent, and provides copies of the interview questions and the consent form. I made a similar request to the executive committee of St. Margaret's Hospital. The approval process took several months; applications were filed in November, 1986, and I received permission to carry out the study in February 1987. Part of the approval process involved attending meetings with social workers and administrators, including a meeting with the chief of obstetrics and gynecology who supervises adolescent services to explain the goals of the study. Brigham and Women's Hospital requires that the principal investigator of any study involving patients be on the hospital staff; the associate director of social services agreed to be principal investigator.

Participation in the study was voluntary. Social workers were appropriately protective of the young mothers who were to be subjects and wanted assurances that the research would not exploit or harm them. To assure that no potential subjects felt pressured to participate, the social workers informed mothers about the study but, in keeping with the Human Subjects Review Committee guidelines, did not persuade them to participate or formally obtain their consent. At the beginning of each interview session, I gave the respondent a copy of the consent form, read the form to the participant, and obtained her signature. Each participant kept a copy of the consent form. The thirty interviewees were each paid $20 for participating in the study. Funding was provided by a grant from the Massachusetts Maternity and Foundling Hospital Corporation.

Appendix B: Sample Research Request Form

Sample Research Consent Form

```
                        BRIGHAM AND WOMEN'S HOSPITAL

                          Research Consent Form

                                (Revised)
```

Date prepared:_____2/9/87_____   Approved for Use by the Brigham and Women's
                                            Hospital Human Research Committee on:
Project Title:___UNDERSTANDING THE_____   2/12/87
__MEANING OF SECOND BIRTHS TO BLACK___   _____
__TEEN MOTHERS_____
Principal Investigator and   Signed by:_____
Co-Investigator(s):__Anne Groves,__   Secretary, Human Research Committee
__Assoc. Director of Social Service__
__Constance W. Williams, Heller School,   Protocol Number:_____86-1975-1_____
__Brandeis University_____
                                            Expiration Date:_____12/15/87_____

We would like permission to enroll you as a participant in a research study. The
purpose of this study is to find out more about young mothers and their ideas and
feelings about pregnancy and motherhood. Much of what is known about the experience of teen mothers is based on what others think. This interview will focus on
your thoughts and feelings about pregnancy and motherhood. The reasons I am asking these questions is to provide information that will help others improve services and programs that are now available and to develop new policies and programs
to better meet the needs of teen parents.

Participation in this study requres one interview, approximately two hours in
length. This face-to-face interview will take place in your home, the adolescent
clinic, or in a place of your choice.

The following paragraphs contain standard information which, in the opinion of the
Human Research Committee of the Brigham and Women's Hospital, generally applies to
persons involved in a research study and are required on all consent forms.

In the event that any time during the course of this study, you feel you have not
been adequately informed as to the risks, benefits, or your rights as a research
subject, or feel under excessive duress to continue in this study against your
wishes, the Executive Secretary of the Human Research Committee, or a representa-
tive, is available to speak to you at (732-5740). If you have specific questions
about the interview, the Associate Director of Social Service, Anne Groves, may be
reached at (732-6465).

You will be paid $20 for one interview.

Confidential information contained in your medical record may not be furnished to
anyone unaffiliated with the Brigham and Women's Hospital without your written consent, except as required by law or regulation.

Your name or any other identifying information will not be used. Interviews will be
identified by a code number.

You are free to withdraw your consent and to discontinue participation in this study
at any time, and such discontinuance will not affect your regular treatments or
medical care or social services in any way.

A signed copy of this consent form will be made available to you.

Sample Research Consent Form Continued

RESEARCH CONSENT FORM

I have fully explained the procedures and their purpose. I have asked whether or not any questions have arisen regarding the interview process or any other aspect of this study and have answered them to the best of my ability. I have explained that participation is voluntary and confidential.

_____   _____
DATE   RESPONSIBLE INVESTIGATOR

I have been fully informed as to the procedure to be followed in the interview process. I have been informed as to the purpose of this study. In signing this consent form, I agree to be interviewed and I understand that I am free to withdraw my consent and discontinue my participation at any time. I understand that if I have any questions at any time, they will be answered.

_____   _____
DATE   PATIENT

THIS CONSENT FORM WAS PROVIDED BY THE BRIGHAM AND WOMEN'S HOSPITAL

Appendix C:
Sample Interview Guide

INTERVIEW SCHEDULE   MAPPS I.D. No._____
                                            Location_____
(to be administered by   Date_____

INTRODUCTION:

        Hello, my name is Connie Williams. You remember from the letter you
received and your conversation with _____ that we are trying to
find out more about young mothers and their ideas and feelings about pregnancy
and motherhood. Much of what is known about the experience of teen mothers is
based on what others think. This interview will focus on your thoughts and
feelings about pregnancy and motherhood. The reason I am asking these
questions is to provide information that will help others improve services and
programs that are now available and develop new programs to better meet the
needs of teen parents. Do you have any questions about the study or this
interview?

        Now I want to make sure you understand your rights before we proceed with
the interview.

        (Consent Form is read and interpreted to respondent. All questions are
        answered and respondents' signature is obtained.)

        Let's go ahead with the interview. Remember that you have the right not
to answer any question that makes you feel uncomfortable.

First, let me ask you a few questions about your child(ren).

 1. What was the date of your first child's birth?

     _____   _____   _____
         Month   Day   Year

 2. Is first child a girl or a boy?

     _____girl

     _____boy

 3. First child's name? _____   (WRITE FIRST NAME ONLY)

 4. How much did _____ (baby's name) weigh when s(he) was born?

                   _____lbs.   _____oz

THIS INTERVIEW SCHEDULE IS BASED ON THE CHILD WELFARE LEAGUE OF
AMERICA (CWLA) INTERVIEW GUIDES DESIGNED FOR THE 1983 CWLA STUDY
CONDUCTED BY SHELBY H. MILLER. THE SOURCE FOR THE INTERVIEW GUIDES
IS THE CWLA LIBRARY.

5. Was _____ (baby's name) full-term or premature?

   _____full-term

   _____premature (anything < 9 months)

   (If premature)
   About how early was s(he)?

   _____weeks (FILL IN ACTUAL NUMBER)

   _____don't know

6. Tell me your date of birth.

   _____   _____   _____
       Month   Day   Year

7. How old were you when _____ (baby's name) was born?

   _____years old

8. Now I want you to think back to when _____ was born. How do
   you remember feeling and thinking about being a mother?

   _____

   _____

   _____

   _____

   ____

9. Tell me what it's like being a mother now. Can you describe what it means
   to you?

   _____

   _____

10. Would you say that your first pregnancy was <u>very easy</u>, <u>somewhat easy</u>,
    <u>somewhat difficult</u>, <u>very difficult</u>.

    _____very easy

    _____somewhat easy

    _____somewhat difficult

    _____very difficult

(IF INTERVIEWEE IS MOTHER OF ONE CHILD, SKIP TO QUESTION 19)

Now I want to ask the same questions about your second child and second pregnancy.

11. What was the date of your second child's birth?

_____   _____   _____
     Month   Day   Year

12. Is your second child a girl or boy?

_____girl

_____boy

13. Second child's name? _____ (WRITE FIRST NAME ONLY)

14. How much did _____ (baby's name) weigh when s(he) was born?

_____lbs.   _____oz.

15. Was _____ (baby's name) full-term or premature?

_____full-term

_____premature (anything < 9 months)

(If premature)
About how early was s(he)?

_____weeks (FILL IN ACTUAL NUMBERS)

_____don't know

16. How old were you when _____ (baby's name) was born?

_____years old

17. Think back to when _____ was born.

How do you remember feeling and thinking about being a mother?

_____

_____

_____

_____

18. Would you say that your second pregnancy was <u>very easy</u>, <u>somewhat easy</u>, somewhat difficult, <u>very difficult</u>.

_____very easy

_____somewhat easy

_____somewhat difficult

_____very difficult

These next questions are about your living arrangements.

19. Who do you and ___(name child(ren)___ live with?

(LIST ALL PERSONS IN HOUSEHOLD)

Relation to Respondent	Age
_____	____
_____	____
_____	____
_____	____
_____	____
_____	____
_____	____

20. Are these the same people you were living with when you became pregnant with _____ (first baby's name)?

_____yes   _____no

21. Are these the same people you were living with when you became pregnant with _____ (second baby's name)?

_____yes   _____no

(IF NO ASK):

22. How are things different? (LIST ALL PERSONS IN HOUSEHOLD)

FIRST PREGNANCY	SECOND PREGNANCY
_____	_____
_____	_____
_____	_____

23. Have you moved in the last two years? _____yes _____no

    Number of moves _____

24. How long have you been at the address you have now?

    _____years   _____months

25. With whom have you lived for most of your life:
    (SELECT ONE ANSWER)

    ___mother only

    ___father only

    ___both parents

    ___other relative (Specify) _____

    ___guardian (Elaborate)_____

    ___institution (Specify)_____

    ___Foster homes (if yes) How many? _____ when? _____

    ___other (Specify)_____

The next series of questions are about your family.

    IF FATHER NOT MENTIONED IN #19 ASK:

26. Tell me about your father. (Let respondent talk about her father)
    (PROBES: Married to mother, current marital status, degree of contact,
             location, father of siblings, etc)

    _____

    _____

    _____

    _____

27. You were _____yrs. old when your first child was born. Do you know how
    old your mother was when she had her first baby?

            _____yes   How old was she?_____

            _____no

<u>(ASK NEXT QUESTION IF RESPONDENT NOT FIRST CHILD)</u>

28. How old was your mother when you were born?

    _____yrs. old

    _____don't know

Now, tell me about your relatives near your own age (sisters or cousins).

29. Do you have a sister who became pregnant as a teenager?

    Yes_____   No_____

    a. If yes, How did she resolve the pregnancy?

    _____

    _____

30. At what age was she pregnant? _____

31. What about cousins or friends? (Get ages of cousins or friends with
    children or pregnant)

    _____

    _____

    _____

    _____

    _____

    _____

Now, I want to ask about school.

32. Tell me the last grade you completed.

    _____

33. Are you currently in school?

    _____yes   _____Grade   _____GED   _____Other

    _____no   (IF ANSWER IS NO, SKIP TO QUESTION 37)

34. Who takes care of the baby when you are in school?

    ___ baby's maternal grandmother

    ___other relative   (Specify)_____

    ___baby's paternal grandmother

    ___baby's father

    ___day care center

    ___family day care

    ___other   (Specify)_____

35. How did you feel when you went back to school after you had your baby?

    _____

    _____

36. How does your family feel about your being in school, now that you have a
    baby to care for? (PROBE TO SEE IF FAMILY ENCOURAGES OR DISCOURAGES
    SCHOOL ATTENDANCE)

    _____

    _____

    _____

(IF NOT IN SCHOOL ASK Q. 37-40)

37. Why aren't you in school?

    ___don't like/don't want to go

    ___no child care

    ___couldn't get readmitted

    ___other

38. When did you leave school? (GET NUMBER OF MONTHS EITHER BEFORE OR AFTER)

    ___months before birth

    ___months after birth

39. Why did you leave school? (UNDERLINE: CHECK ALL THAT APPLY)

___didn't like it

___got pregnant

___had to care for baby

___other (Specify)_____

40. Do you plan to return to school?

___yes   (If yes)   When?

___no   ___next semester

                          ___in about a year

                          ___in about 2 years

                          ___more than 2 years

                          ___don't know

(ALL RESPONDENTS)

41. Did you ever attend a special school program before or after your child(ren)s birth?

___Yes   ___No

First child   Second Child
___before birth   ___before birth

___after birth   ___after birth

___no. of months   ___no. of months

_____

42. If you had your wish, how far would you ideally like to go in school?

___6-8 grades   ___B.A degree

___9-11 grades   ___graduate or prof. school

___12th grade   ___other (Specify)_____

___junior college   _____

43. How far do you <u>really</u> think you'll be able to go in school?

    ___6-8 grades   ___B.A. degree

    ___9-11 grades   ___graduate or professional school

    ___12th grade   ___Other (Specify)_____

    ___junior college   _____

44. How far does your mother expect you to go?_____

    How far does your father expect you to go?_____

45. In what ways is school important to you? (Check all that apply.)

    _____place to see friends

    _____it gives me something to do

    _____structured learning environment

    _____only a diploma (i.e., means to future goal)

    _____Other _____

46. How about your parents? How far did your parents go in school?
(GET HIGHEST GRADE EACH OF THEM FINISHED)

      _____father   _____mother

47. Did either of your parents get any other schooling or training such as business or trade school?

    ___yes (if yes)   a) which Parent?_____

    ___no   b) what kind of training?_____

In this next group of questions I'll be asking about the ways you think of yourself.

48. Who in your family are you most like? (list in order given by respondent)

    Father   _____
    Mother   _____
    Brother (Age)   _____
    Sister (Age)   _____
    Other   _____

49. What about you is similar to that person?

_____

_____

50. Do you identify strongly, somewhat strongly, a little, or not at all with that person? (PROBE: How or in what ways?)

_____strongly

_____somewhat strongly

_____a little

_____not at all

51. Can you say who has been the most important (influential) person in your life? Tel me about that person.

_____

_____

_____

52. How would that person describe you?

_____bright/smart

_____friendly/good/nice

_____funny/crazy

_____kind/generous

_____negative attributes   (Specify)_____

_____Other

(GO TO NEXT PAGE AND READ SELF-ESTEEM QUESTIONS TO RESPONDENT)

53. <u>SELF-ESTEEM QUESTIONS</u>*
        I'm now going to read you a list of things people sometimes say about
     themselves. I want you to tell me if you:
            1. <u>agree strongly</u> that the statement describes you
            2. just <u>agree</u> that the statement describes you
            3. <u>disagree</u> that the statement describes you
            4. <u>disagree strongly</u> that the statement describes you
(REPEAT 4 CATEGORIES. THEN READ EACH STATEMENT. IF NECESSARY PROBE WITH ALL CATEGORIES.)

	agree strongly	agree	disagree	disagree strongly
53- 1. I feel that I'm a person of worth at least on an equal basis with others.				
53- 2. There are lots of things about myself I'd change if I could.				
53- 3. I'm a lot of fun to be with.				
53- 4. Other people who are important to me really accept me.				
53- 5. Most people my own age are more satisfied with themselves than I am with myself.				
53- 6. I feel I do not have much to be proud of.				
53- 7. I often feel pushed around by others.				
53- 8. I'm pretty sure of myself.				
53- 9. I'm easy to like.				
53-10. I can't be depended on.				
53-11. I'm popular with people my own age.				
53-12. I certainly feel helpless at times.				
53-13. Things usually don't bother me.				
53-14. Most people who are important to me, who know me, think I do most things well.				
53-15. I often wish I was someone else.				
53-16. I would rather be supported for the rest of my life than work.				
53-17. I am proud of my body.				
53-18. The picture I have of myself in the future satisfies me.				

*Miller, Shelby H., <u>Children as Parents</u>, page 22.
    Coopersmith items 2,3,4,7,8,9,10,11,13,15
    Rosenberg items 1,5,6,12,14

The next questions have to do with jobs and other ways people get money to live on.

54. Do you have a job now? (<u>JOBS=ANY WORK YOUNG MOTHER GETS PAID FOR</u>)

   ___yes (If yes)   a) What king of job do you have?_____

                                b) _____

                                    How many hours a week do you work?_____

                                  c) Who takes care of _____ when you are working

                ___baby's maternal grandmother

                ___other relative (Specify)_____

                ___baby's paternal grandmother

                ___baby's father

                ___day care center

                ___family day care

                ___neighbor

                ___other (Specify)_____

55. How about five years from now when you are _____? Do you think you'll be working then?

                                  ___yes

                                  ___no

(IF NO, ASK)
55a. Why not? ___will be in school

                    ___will be caring for her children

                    ___don't want to work

                    ___other

56. Now I'm going to read you a list of ways many people get money to live on. Can you tell me if your family gets any money from: (<u>READ LIST AND CHECK ALL THAT APPLY</u>)

   ___your mother's job   ___AFDC

   ___your father's job   ___parent's unemployment compensation

   ___your own job   ___parent's veteran's benefits

   ___your other relatives   ___parent's social security

   ___the baby's father   ___other (Specify)_____

   ___the baby's father's family _____

57. Of all your family members, who would you say is the most helpful to you?

_____

_____

58. Name the ways in which that family member has been helpful.
    (CHECK ALL THAT APPLY)

    ___babysitting   ___talking/emotional support

    ___financial help   ___transportation

    ___material items (clothes, toys)   ___other (Specify)_____

59. Who makes most of the decisions in your family?

    _____

60. How do you fit into the decision-making process? (Give example) For
    example, if your child(ren) had pretty bad colds and you had to go out,
    who would decide whether you should go?

    _____

    _____

The next questions are about your personal feelings about specific times in
your life.

61. Do you remember a time or an event when you felt great about yourself?
    Describe that time for me.

    _____

    _____

62. How did you feel when you first found out you were pregnant?

    _____

    _____

63. Who was the first person you confided in as soon as you knew you were
    pregnant?

    _____

64. How did this person react?

_____

(IF PERSON CONFIDED IN WAS NOT RESPONDENT'S MOTHER, ASK THE FOLLOWING QUESTION)

65. How did your mother react?

_____

66. Just before you became pregnant the first time, did you want to become pregnant when you did? (ALLOW RESPONDENT TO ELABORATE)

_____Pregnancy intended   _____Pregnancy unintended

_____

_____

67. Did you consider having an abortion or giving the baby up for adoption?

___no

___considered abortion

___considered adoption

___considered both

___don't know/don't remember

68. What about the father of the baby? Was he involved in your decision-making?

_____yes   _____no

(IF YES, ASK THE FOLLOWING QUESTION)

69. Did he encourage or discourage you to have the baby?

_____

_____

70. Did he make any promises about what he would do if you decided to have the baby? (check all that apply)

___accompany you to the delivery room

___visit in the hospital

___help out financially

___babysit

___get married

___other (Specify) _____

71. Were you or your boyfriend doing anything to prevent getting pregnant when you became pregnant the first time?

___yes   (If yes) What?_____

___no   (If no ask next question)

(IF RESPONDENT HAS ONE CHILD SKIP TO QUESTION 82)   (72-81 FOR SECOND BIRTH ONLY)

72. How did you feel when you found out you were pregnant a second time?

_____

_____

73. Who was the first person you confided in as soon as you knew you were pregnant a second time?

_____

74. How did this person react?

_____

(IF PERSON CONFIDED IN WAS NOT RESPONDENT'S MOTHER, ASK THE FOLLOWING QUESTION)

75. How did your mother react?

_____

76. Just before you became pregnant with your second baby, did you want to become pregnant when you did? (ALLOW RESPONDENT TO ELABORATE)

_____Pregnancy intended   _____Pregnancy unintended

_____

_____

77. Did you consider having an abortion or giving the second baby up for adoption?

___no

___considered abortion

___considered adoption

___considered both

___don't know/don't remember

78. What about the father of the second baby? Was he involved in your decision-making?

_____yes   _____no

(IF YES, ASK THE FOLLOWING QUESTION)

79. Did he encourage or discourage you to have the baby?

_____

_____

80. Did he make any promises about what he would do if you decided to have the baby? (check all that apply)

___accompany you to the delivery room

___visit in the hospital

___help out financially

___babysit

___get married

___other (Specify) _____

81. Were you or your boyfriend doing anything to prevent getting pregnant when you became pregnant the second time?

___yes   (If yes) What?_____

___no   (If no ask next question)

82. I am going to read some reasons why some people don't use birth control.
    Tell me which ones apply to you.

    ___don't want to plan sex

    ___too much trouble

    ___only have sex when I think I'm safe

    ___don't know when I'm going to have sex

    ___don't know where to get birth control

    ___don't know what to use

    ___worried about side effects/nothing is safe

    ___it's too embarrassing

    ___don't want to (PROBE WHY NOT)_____

    ___boyfriend doesn't want to use anything

    ___I did not think I would get pregnant

    ___didn't mind taking a chance

    ___other (Specify)_____

83. What are you doing now to keep from getting pregnant?

    _____

    _____

    _____

Now I would like to ask you a few questions about _____'s father.

84. First of all, are you in contact with him?

    ___yes, live together   ___no contact

    ___yes, but don't live together

    How often do you see him?

    ___every day

    ___several times a week

    ___once a week

    ___once a month

    ___less than once a month

85. How would you describe your relationship to him? (PROBE) (comes to see baby only, still going out with him, etc)

_____

_____

86. Is he in school?   ___yes   ___no

87. What is the last grade he completed? _____

88. Is he working?   ___yes   ___no   ___don't know

89. Does he give you any financial help?   ___yes   ___no

90. Are there other ways in which he helps you?

_____

91. How old is he now? _____

(IF THERE IS A SECOND CHILD WITH A DIFFERENT FATHER THAN THE FIRST, REPEAT ABOVE QUESTIONS) (IF RESPONDENT HAS ONE CHILD, SKIP TO QUESTION 101)

92. Tell me about the father of your second child?

_____

_____

93. First of all, are you in contact with him?

___yes, live together   ___no contact

___yes, but don't live together

How often do you see him?

___every day

___several times a week

___once a week

___once a month

___less than once a month

94. How would you describe your relationship to him? (PROBE)   (comes to see
    baby only, still going out with him, etc)

    _____

    _____

95. Is he in school?   ___yes   ___no

96. What is the last grade he completed? _____

97. Is he working?   ___yes   ___no   ___don't know

98. Does he give you any financial help?   ___yes   ___no

99. Are there other ways in which he helps you?

    _____

100. How old is he now? _____

101. The next statements are about beliefs. I would like to know how you feel
     about these statements.

	agree strongly	agree	disagree	disagree strongly
a. A girl becomes a woman by having a baby.				
b. I was treated more independently after my baby was born.				
c. More children make for a happier household.				
d. A girl is more attractive when she is pregnant.				
e. Childbearing is the most important thing a woman does.				
f. On the whole, children give more pleasure than trouble.				
g. It's best not to be an only child.				
h. A woman and her children are a complete family.				

Now I want to ask a few questions about services.

102. What services are you currently receiving?

___medical   ___birth control counseling

___social services (counseling)

___WIC

___job training

___other

103. Are you associated with any organizations in your community? For example the YWCA, or a church? (PROBE)

_____

_____

The last questions have to do with the future

104. First, what would you like to be doing 5 years from now?
     (MAKE SUGGESTIONS ONLY IF RESPONDENT HAS GREAT DIFFICULTY RESPONDING)

_____

_____

_____

105. Do you have plans to get married in the future?

     ___yes   ___no

Ask respondent to elaborate.

_____

_____

106. Do you want to have more children?

     ___yes   ___no

If yes, How many _____ and how old would you like to be when your last child is born?_____

107. Tell me what your ambitions are for your child(ren).

_____

_____

108. Do you think you'll be able to make those ambitions come true?

109. If a 16 year old girl told you she wanted a baby, what advise would you give her?

_____

_____

110. What choices (options) did you see yourself having before you became pregnant?

_____

_____

111. What options do you see yourself having now?

_____

_____

That's all the questions I have except I'm curious about your reactions to the interview.

112. Were there any questions you did not want to answer?

___yes (if yes) Which questions _____

                                   _____

___no

Thank you very much for your time and cooperation. I don't think I would need to, but just in case I find something unclear as I go over the interview, would it be O.K. if I called you to check out the information?

PHONE NO._____

ADDRESS_____

        _____

Notes

1. CBS, January 25, 1986.
2. National Center for Health Statistics, 1983.
3. National Center for Health Statistics, 1983.
4. National Center for Health Statistics, 1983.
5. National Center for Health Statistics, 1983.
6. Speech, "The National Crisis of Teenage Pregnancy." Ford Hall Forum, Boston, Mass. Nov 3, 1985.
7. Kathleen Teltsch, "Teen-Age mothers get aid in study," *New York Times,* May 19, 1985, p. 27.
8. *Boston Globe,* October 22, 1985, p. 28.
9. This research used the *Cognitive and Emotional Development, 1975–77.* Data set (made accessible, 1980, raw data file). These data were collected by M. Horner and are available through the archives of The Henry A. Murray Research Center of Radcliffe College, Cambridge, Mass. (Producer and Distributer).
10. Deborah Kline Walker, *Draft Interview for Mothers and Grandmothers,* Harvard School of Public Health, Cambridge, Mass., 1986.
11. Boston Redevelopment Authority, 1988.
12. Susan Hartman, *New York Times,* January 12, 1989, p. C1; Jane Meredith Adams, *Boston Globe,* February 6, 1989, p. 2.
13. *New York Times,* January 24, 1990, p. B6.

References

Anderson, E. 1978. *A Place on the Corner*. Chicago: University of Chicago Press.

Ayala, G., and R. E. McAnarney. 1983. Parenthood in two Subcultures: White, middle-class couples and black, low-income adolescents in Rochester, New York. *Adolescence* 18 (no. 71): 595–608.

Baldwin, W. H. 1985. Trends and correlates of adolescent pregnancy and childbearing in the U.S. Statement made before the U.S. Congress, House Subcommittee on Census and Population, 30 April 1985.

Bane, M. J. 1986a. Household composition and poverty. In *Fighting Poverty: What Works and What Doesn't*, edited by S.H. Danziger, 209–231. Cambridge, Massachusetts: Harvard University Press.

Bane, M. J. 1986b. Welfare: Is it part of the problem or solution? Paper presented at Prevention: Speakout '86, National Conference of the Children's Defense Fund, 26–28 February, Washington, D.C.

Bane, M. J., and D. Ellwood. 1983. *Slipping Into and Out of Poverty: The Dynamics of Spells*. Cambridge, Massachusetts: National Bureau of Economic Research (working paper no. 1199).

Belenky, M. C. Blythe, N. Goldberger, and J. Tarule. 1986. *Women's Ways of Knowing: The Development of Self, Voice, and Mind*. New York: Basic Books.

Bell, W. 1965. *Aid to Dependent Children*. New York: Columbia University Press.

Billingsley, A. 1968. *Black Families in White America*. Englewood Cliffs, New Jersey: Prentice Hall.

Brooks-Gunn, J., and F. F. Furstenberg, Jr. 1986. The children of adolescent mothers: Physical, academic, and psychological outcomes. *Developmental Review* 6: 224–251.

Bruner, J. 1986a. *Actual Minds, Possible Worlds*. Cambridge, Massachusetts: Harvard University Press.

Bruner, J. 1986b. Life as narrative. Paper presented at the Susan Wise Lecture, New School for Social Research. Formal edition reprinted in *Social Research* 54 (no. 1): 13–32.

Cherlin, A. J. 1981. *Marriage, Divorce, Remarriage*. Cambridge, Massachusetts: Harvard University Press.

Children's Defense Fund. 1987. *Declining Earnings of Young Men: Their Relation to Poverty, Teen Pregnancy, and Family Formation.* Washington, D.C.: CDF Adolescent Pregnancy Prevention Clearinghouse.

Coles, R., and G. Stokes. 1985. *Sex and the American Teenager.* New York: Harper & Row.

Coopersmith, S. 1967. *The Antecedents of Self-Esteem.* San Francisco: W.H. Freeman and Co.

Cutright, P. 1972a. Illegitimacy in the United States: 1920-1968. in *Demographic and Social Aspects of Population Growth,* edited by C.F. Westoff and R. Parke, 375–438. Washington, D.C.: Government Printing Office.

Cutright, P. 1972b. Stigmatized from birth. Review of *Illegitimacy: Law and Social Policy,* by H. D. Krause. In *Family Planning Perspectives* 4 (no. 2): 58.

Cutright, P. 1973. Illegitimacy and income supplements. In *Studies in Public Welfare.* 93d Cong., 1st sess., paper no. 12, pt. 1. Washington, D.C.: Government Printing Office.

Danziger, S., and D. H. Weinberg, eds. 1986. *Fighting Poverty: What Works and What Doesn't.* Cambridge, Massachusetts: Harvard University Press.

David, H. P. 1972. Unwanted pregnancies: Costs and alternatives. In *Demographic and Social Aspects of Population Growth,* edited by C.F. Westoff and R. Parke. Washington, D.C.: Government Printing Office.

Davis, K. 1972. The American family in relation to demographic change. In *Adolescent Pregnancy and Childbearing: Findings from Research,* edited by C. S. Chilman. Washington D.C.: Government Printing Office.

Donzelot, J. 1979. *The Policing of Families.* New York: Pantheon Books.

Edelman, M. 1987. *Families in Peril: An Agenda for Social Change.* Cambridge, Massachusetts: Harvard University Press.

Erikson, E. 1968. *Identity, Youth, and Crisis.* New York: W.W. Norton.

Ford, K. 1983. Second pregnancies among teenage mothers. *Family Planning Perspectives* (November/December): 268–272.

Forrest, J D. 1987. Unintended pregnancy among American women. *Family Planning Perspectives* 19: 76–77.

Foster, S. E. 1986. *Preventing Teenage Pregnancy: A Public Policy Guide.* Washington, D.C.: Council of State Policy and Planning Agencies.

Frazier, E. F. 1966. *The Negro Family in the United States.* Chicago: University of Chicago Press.

Furstenberg, F. F., Jr. 1976. *Unplanned Parenthood: The Social Consequences of Teenage Childbearing.* New York: Free Press.

Furstenberg, F. F., Jr. 1980. The social consequences of teenage parenthood. In *Adolescent Pregnancy and Childbearing: Findings from research,* edited by C. Chilman. Washington, D.C.: Government Printing Office.

Furstenberg, Frank. F., Jr., Brooks-Gunn, J., and Morgan, S. Philip. (1987). *Adolescent mothers in later life.* Cambridge, England: Cambridge University Press.

Garfinkel, I., and S. McLanahan. 1986. *Single Mothers and Their Children: A New American Dilemma.* Washington, D.C.: Urban Institute Press.

Gilder, G. 1982. *Wealth and Poverty.* New York: Bantam Books.

Gilligan, C. 1982. *In a Different Voice.* Cambridge, Massachusetts: Harvard University Press.

Glaser, B. G., and A. L. Strauss. 1967. *The Discovery of Grounded Theory: Strategies for Qualitative Research.* New York: Aldine De Gruyter.

Goode, W. J. 1960. Illegitimacy in the Caribbean social structure. *American Sociological Review* 25 (no. 2): 21–30.

Goode, W. J. 1964. Illegitimacy, anomie, and cultural penetration. In *Readings on the Family and Society,* edited by W.J. Goode, 38–55. Englewood Cliffs, New Jersey: Prentice Hall.

Goode, W. J. 1982. *The Family.* Englewood Cliffs, N.J.: Prentice Hall.

Gorbach, J. A., D. K. Walker, and H. Ruch-Ross. 1986. *Massachusetts Adolescent Pregnant and Parenting System.* Massachusetts Department of Public Health.

Gutman, H. G. 1976. *The Black Family in Slavery and Freedom, 1750–1925.* New York: Pantheon.

Hayes, C. D. 1987. *Risking The Future: Adolescent Sexuality, Pregnancy, and Childbearing,* vol. 1. Washington, D.C.: National Academy Press.

Hill, R. 1972. *The Strengths of Black Families.* New York: Emerson Hall Publishers.

Hofferth, S. L. and C. D. Hayes. 1987. *Risking the Future: Adolescent Sexuality, Pregnancy, and Childbearing,* vol. 2. Washington, D.C.: National Academy Press.

Hogan, D. P., and E. M. Kitagawa. 1985. The impact of social status, family structure, and neighborhood on the fertility of black adolescents. *American Journal of Sociology* 90 (no. 4): 825–855.

Horowitz, R. 1983. *Honor and the American Dream.* New Brunswick, New Jersey: Rutgers University Press.

Jackson, M. R. 1984. *Self-Esteem and Meaning: A Life-Investigation Historical.* Albany: State University of New York Press.

Joe, T. 1987. The other side of black female-headed families: The status of adult black men. *Family Planning Perspectives* 19: 74–76.

Joffe, C. 1986. *The Regulation of Sexuality Experiences of Family Planning Workers.* Philadelphia: Temple University Press.

Jones, E., J. D. Forrest, S. K. Henshaw, J. Silverman, and S. Torres. 1988. Unintended pregnancy, contraceptive practice and family planning services in developed countries. *Family Planning Perspectives.* 20: 53–67.

Jones, E., J. D. Forrest, N. Goldman, et al. 1985. Teenage pregnancy in developed countries: Determinants and policy implications. *Family Planning Perspectives* 17 (March/April): 53–63.

Ladner, J. 1986. Teenage pregnancy: The implications for black Americans. In *The State of Black America, 1986,* edited by J.D. Williams, 65–84. New York: National Urban League.

Lasch, C. 1977. *Haven in a Heartless World.* New York: Basic Books.

Lemann, N. 1986. The origins of the underclass. *Atlantic Monthly* 257 (no. 6): 31–55.

Levy, S. D., with W. J. Grinker. 1983. *Choices and Life Circumstances: An Ethnographic Study of Project Redirection Teens*. New York: Manpower Demonstration Research Corporation.

Liebow, E. 1967. *Tally's Corner: A Study of Negro Streetcorner Men*. Boston, Massachusetts: Little Brown.

Luker, K. 1975. *Taking Chances: Abortion and the Decision Not to Contracept*. Berkeley: University of California Press.

McLanahan, S., and L. Bumpass. 1988. Intergenerational consequences of family disruption. *American Journal of Sociology* 94 (no. 1): 130–152.

MacLeod, J. 1987. *Ain't No Making It: Leveled Aspirations in a Low-Income Neighborhood*. Boulder, Colorado: Westview Press.

Marini, M. Mooney. 1984. Age and sequencing norms in the transition to Adulthood. *Social Forces* 63: 1.

Martin, E. P., and J. Martin. 1978. *The Black Extended Family*. Chicago: University of Chicago Press.

Mead, L. M. 1986. *Beyond Entitlement: The Social Obligations of Citizenship*. New York: Free Press.

Miller, S. H. 1983. *Children as Parents: A Study of Childbearing and Child Rearing Among 12-to 15-Year-Olds*. Washington, D.C.: Child Welfare League of America.

Mills, C. Wright. 1959. *The Sociological Imagination*. New York: Oxford University Press.

Mishler, E. G. 1986. *Research Interviewing: Context and Narrative*. Cambridge, Massachusetts: Harvard University Press.

Moore, K. A., and M. R. Burt. 1982. *Private Crisis, Public Cost*. Washington, D.C.: Urban Institute.

Moore, K. A., M. Simms, and C. Betsey. 1986. *Choice and Circumstance*. Rutgers, New Jersey: Transaction, Inc.

Moynihan, D. P. 1965. *The Negro Family: The Case for National Action*. Washington, D.C.: Office of Policy Planning and Research, U.S. Department of Labor.

Moynihan, D. P. 1986. *Family and Nation*. Cambridge, Massachusetts: Harvard University Press.

Murray, C. A. 1984. *Losing Ground: American Social Policy, 1950–1980*. New York: Basic Books.

Muuss, R. E. 1982. *Theories of Adolescence*. New York: Random House.

Newberger, C. M. 1977. *Parental Conceptions of Children and Child Rearing: A Structural-Developmental Analysis*. Ph.D. diss., Harvard University.

Newberger, C. M., and S. J. Cook. 1983. Parental awareness and child abuse and neglect: A cognitive developmental analysis of urban and rural samples. *American Journal of Orthopsychiatry* 53: 512–524.

Novak, M. 1987. *The New Consensus on Family and Welfare*. Washington, D.C.: American Enterprise Institute for Public Policy Research.

Pearce, D. 1978. The feminization of poverty: Women, work, and welfare. *Urban Social Change Review* 11: 28–36.

Pittman, K., and G. Adams. 1988. *Teenage Pregnancy: An Advocate's Guide To The Numbers*. Washington, D.C.: Children's Defense Fund Adolescent Pregnancy Prevention Clearinghouse.

Polit, D., J. Kahn, D. Stevens. 1985. *Final Impacts From ProjectsRedirection*. New York: Manpower Demonstration Research Corporation.

Presser, H. B. 1980. Sally's corner: Coping with Unmarried motherhood. *Journal of Social Issues* 36 (no. 1): 107–129.

Quinn, W., N. Newfield, and H. Protinsky. 1985. Rites of passage in families with adolescents. *Family Process* 24: 101–111.

Rainwater, L., and W. L. Yancey. 1967. *The Moynihan Report and the Politics of Controversy*. Cambridge, Massachusetts: M.I.T. Press.

Rainwater, L., and K. Weinstein. 1974. *And the Poor Get Children: Sex, Contraception, and Family Planning in the Working Class*. New York: Franklin Watts.

Rosenberg, M. 1965 *Society and the Adolescent Self-Image*. Princeton, New Jersey: Princeton University Press.

Rosoff, J. I. 1988. Not just teenagers (editorial). *Family Planning Perspectives*. 20 (no. 2): 52.

Ross, H. L., and I. V. Sawhill. 1975. *Time of Transition: The Growth of Families Headed by Women*. Washington, D.C.: Urban Institute.

Schneider, J. W., and P. Conrad. 1983. *Having Epilepsy: The Experience and Control of Illness*. Philadelphia, Pennsylvania: Temple University Press.

Schorr, L. B., with D. Schorr. 1988. *Within Our Reach: Breaking the Cycle of Disadvantage*. New York: Anchor Press/Doubleday.

Schwab, B. 1983. *Someone to Always be There: Teenage Childbearing as Adaptive Strategy in Rural New England*. Ph.D. diss., Brandeis University.

Speraw, S. 1987. Adolescents' perspective of pregnancy: A cross-cultural perspective. *Western Journal of Nursing Research* 9(no. 2): 180–202.

Stack, C. 1974. *All Our Kin: Strategies for Survival in a Black Community*. New York: Harper and Row.

Staples, R., ed. 1971. *The Black Family: Essays and Studies*. Belmont, California: Wadsworth Publishing Co.

Steiner, G. 1981. *The Futility of Family Policy*. Washington, D.C.: Brookings Institute.

Williams, J. D., ed. 1986. *The State of Black America*. New York: National Urban League.

Willie, C. 1976. *A New Look at Black Families*. Bayside, New York: General Hall.

Wilson, W. J. 1987. *The Truly Disadvantaged: The Inner City, the Underclass, and Public Policy*. Chicago: University of Chicago Press.

Zelnik, M., and J. F. Kanter. 1980. Sexual and contraceptive experience of young unmarried women in the United States, 1976 and 1971. In *Adolescent Pregnancy and Childbearing: Findings from Research*, edited by C. Chilman. Washington, D.C.: Government Printing Office.

Zelnik, M., J. F. Kanter, and K. Ford. 1981. *Sex and Pregnancy in Adolescence*. Beverly Hills, California: Sage Publications.

Index

Abortion, xi, 8; black teen rates, 8, 127; contraceptive use and, 25; decision making, 49, 65, 67, 68, 125; parental counseling and, 67, 68–69, 73, 112; U.S. statistics, 11, 12; white teen rate, 3, 8,49, 127

Absent fathers, 27; child support and, 14, 15; family structure affected by, 2; psychological impact of, 71–72, 74; supervision problems and, 60

Adolescent Pregnancy and Parenting Study. *See* Massachusetts Department of Public Health

Adoption, xi, 3, 4, 65, 125

Affirmative action, 29

Age of teen mothers, 8, 23–24, 29, 50 128

Aid to Families with Dependent Children (AFDC), 13, 15; cost of living adjustments, 25; educational attainment and, 75; recipients in study, 54, 55, 80, 113, 114, 115, 130; teen pregnancy and, 17, 22. *See also* Welfare

Alan Guttmacher Institute (AGI), 10, 11, 12

Alliance for Young Families, xi

Baby M case, 33

Baltimore study (Furstenberg), 23, 24, 110, 134

Big sisters, 122, 124

Birth control and contraception, xi, 8; accessibility of, 25; adult rates, 20; first intercourse and, 15; health care institutions and, 110–111, 112, 131; ineffective, 17–21, 24–25, 125, 131–132; male support for, 19; moral issues, 15–16; pill, xi, 18, 20, 110, 112; teen pregnancy affected by, 11–12, 20; U.S. statistics, 11–12. *See also* Prevention strategies for teen pregnancy

Birthrate, xi, 7; age factors, 8, 23–24, 29, 50; black teen, 9, 14, 29, 127, 141–142; cultural factors, 10–12, 20; economic factors, 12–13; illegitimate (out-of-wedlock), 3, 4, 8, 9, 14, 29, 34–35, 36, 128, 129; race factors, 8–10; white teen, 9, 127. *See also* Abortion; First pregnancy; Second pregnancy

Blood, Robert, 2

Boston, MA: black neighborhoods, 116–119, 129; Public Housing, 35; school integration (busing), 104, 107, 133. *See also* Massachusetts Department of Public Health, Adolescent Pregnancy and Parenting Study (MAPPS)

Brigham and Women's Hospital, 44, 111, 122, 123, 139; Adolescent Clinic, 112, 141; Adolescent Reproductive Health Service, 143; Consortium for Pregnant and Parenting Teens, 140

Brown v. Board of Education, 104

Busing. *See* Schools, integration (busing)

About the Author

Constance Willard Williams, Ph.D., is associate professor at the Family and Children's Policy Center, Heller Graduate School for Advanced Studies in Social Welfare, Brandeis University. A social worker with an extensive background in direct practice, public service, and education, Professor Williams has practiced social work in Boston with children and families and has served on the social-work faculties both at Boston University and Boston College. From 1985 to 1987, she was chief policy analyst in Governor Dukakis' Office of Human Resources and directed major human service policy initiatives—among them, the reform of the Commonwealth's child-support enforcement statute. She is co-author with Joe Feagin and Charles Tilly of *Subsidizing the Poor: A Boston Housing Experiment*. Professor Williams has also served as president of the Massachusetts chapter of the National Association of Social Workers (NASW) and as a member of its national board of directors; she is currently chair of the NASW's Communications Committee.